The EPIC OFFICIAL Guide to

Disney CLUB PENGUIN™

ULTIMATE EDITION

by Katherine Noll and Tracey West

Grosset & Dunlap
An Imprint of Penguin Group (USA) Inc.

GROSSET & DUNLAP
Published by the Penguin Group
Penguin Group (USA) Inc., 375 Hudson Street,
New York, New York 10014, USA
Penguin Group (Canada), 90 Eglinton Avenue East, Suite 700,
Toronto, Ontario M4P 2Y3, Canada
(a division of Pearson Penguin Canada Inc.)
Penguin Books Ltd., 80 Strand, London WC2R 0RL, England
Penguin Group Ireland, 25 St. Stephen's Green, Dublin 2, Ireland
(a division of Penguin Books Ltd.)
Penguin Group (Australia), 250 Camberwell Road,
Camberwell, Victoria 3124, Australia
(a division of Pearson Australia Group Pty. Ltd.)
Penguin Books India Pvt. Ltd., 11 Community Centre,
Panchsheel Park, New Delhi–110 017, India
Penguin Group (NZ), 67 Apollo Drive, Rosedale,
Auckland 0632, New Zealand
(a division of Pearson New Zealand Ltd.)
Penguin Books (South Africa) (Pty.) Ltd., 24 Sturdee Avenue,
Rosebank, Johannesburg 2196, South Africa

Penguin Books Ltd., Registered Offices:
80 Strand, London WC2R 0RL, England

ISBN 978-0-448-45844-1   10 9 8 7 6 5 4 3 2 1

Welcome, Penguins!

Hello, and welcome to *The EPIC OFFICIAL Guide to Club Penguin: Ultimate Edition*. The action on Club Penguin moves faster than a group of penguins drilling on the Iceberg! We had to write a new guidebook to keep track of it all. We're happy you are a part of all the excitement on Club Penguin. It's penguins like you who make the island such a fun place to visit.

Whether you are new to the island or have been coming to Club Penguin for a long time, there is something new for every penguin to learn in this guidebook. It's packed with secrets, tips, facts, and other goodies that will make you a Club Penguin expert.

Turn the page and dive in! When you're done flipping through the pages, log in to clubpenguin. com and let us know what you think. We always love to hear what you have to say!

Your friends,
The Club Penguin Team

Table of Contents

Getting Started

Hello, dear reader! As editor in chief of *The Club Penguin Times*, I receive an extraordinary number of questions from penguins every day. I'll make your journey through this book easier by sharing my favorite facts, tips, and secrets.

I'm a Club Penguin Tour Guide. I'll be introducing you to the different sections of this book—and different areas of Club Penguin.

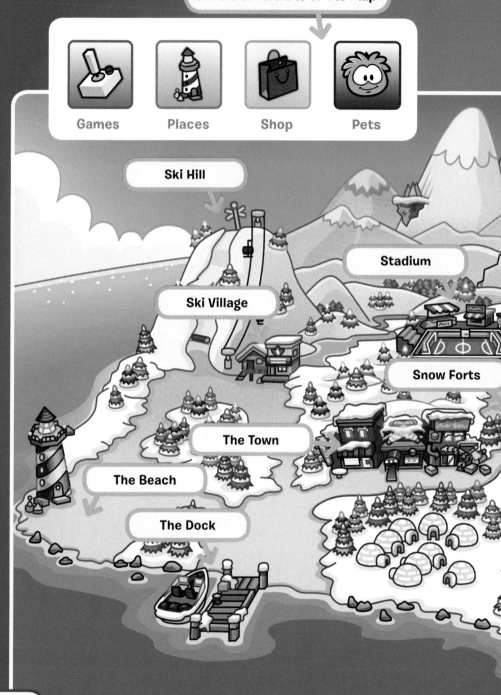

Click on a box to see different versions of the map

Games

Places

Shop

Pets

Ski Hill

Stadium

Ski Village

Snow Forts

The Town

The Beach

The Dock

8

The Map Makes It Easy!

You can get to just about anywhere you want on Club Penguin by waddling around and exploring, but if you're not sure where to go, click on the map on the bottom left of your screen. You'll see a map of Club Penguin with all the major places you can visit. Click on a place and you'll be transported there instantly.

Dojo Courtyard

Mine

The Plaza

Forest

Cove

Games

Are your friends talking about what a great game *Aqua Grabber* is, but you don't know where to find it? No problem! Click on the Games tab on top of the map. Roll over each image with your mouse to see the game title.

Shops

Click on the Shops tab to see places you can shop. In some places you'll find a whole catalog of things to purchase. In other places you'll find special items that you can use when you play a specific game.

Pets

Looking to adopt a puffle? Click on the Pets tab and you're just moments away from being the proud owner of your own furry friend.

Internet Safety First

1. **Always keep personal information to yourself.** Never share it online! That includes your real name, age, address, location, phone number, or school.

2. **Always keep your password safe and private.** Never share it with anyone but your parents or guardian. If you share your password, someone could steal your coins, change your igloo, or get your penguin banned from the site.

3. **Tell a parent if someone says or does something on the Internet that makes you feel uncomfortable.** Also tell them if someone asks you for personal information.

4. **Only visit sites on the Internet that are monitored by moderators.** On Club Penguin, moderators are highly trained members of the staff who monitor behavior and chat. If a penguin says or does something inappropriate, you can report them to a moderator. Click on the penguin, and their Player Card will appear. Choose the 🛡️ to make a report.

Club Penguin Rules

1. Always have fun!

2. Respect other penguins. Do not bully or be mean to other penguins, and don't use inappropriate language or behavior when talking to others.

3. Stay safe online. Don't share personal information like your real name, phone number, address, e-mail, or password.

4. No cheating. Everyone is here to have fun, so follow the rules and play games without using third-party programs.

5. Always help other penguins who are new to Club Penguin and don't know their way around.

If you break any of the rules, you risk being banned from Club Penguin by one of our moderators on staff. This means you will not be able to use your account for a period of time. Sometimes it's for twenty-four hours, or it could be forever. Remember that another player cannot ban you from the site—only a moderator can.

Creating Your Penguin

Many penguins visit Club Penguin every day, but each one is as unique as a snowflake. One of the best things about being a penguin is that you can be whomever you want to be. Here are some things to think about as you create your penguin personality:

• Choose your favorite color to start—then add more colors as you play. You can change colors to match your mood or favorite clothing combo.

• Choose a background for your player card that reflects your interests.

• Use actions like dancing or throwing a snowball to show off your playful side.

• Express your friendly nature by helping other penguins in need.

• Experiment! If you try something and don't like it, just give something else a try.

Your Name

Choosing the right name is important. Once you choose your penguin name, it's yours forever! If a friend asks you for help in choosing a name, try these suggestions:

1. **Never use your real name!** That's a basic rule for Internet safety.

2. **Use your imagination.** Try a made-up name. One penguin we know is named I 8 A B, for example.

3. **Think of your favorite things.** Your favorite animal or sports team could be part of your name.

4. **Add some numbers.** If the name you want is taken, add some numbers to it and make it different. For example: DaisyGirl910. For safety reasons, don't use your birthday or address.

5. **Remember:** Make sure your name is between four and twelve characters long. Once you come up with your name, write it down along with your password. Give this to a parent or guardian and ask them to keep it safe for you, in case you forget.

Create Your Penguin

This is where you can create your penguin's own unique style.

 1.

Create Penguin Name:

Enter Penguin Name

- 4-12 letters, numbers or spaces
- Do not use your real name

Choose a color that reflects your unique style. You can always change your color later whenever you'd like by going to the Penguin Style catalog in the Gift Shop. I've chosen to wear green for as long as I can remember. Some penguins choose to wear different colors for special events, like sports games—or to show what mood they are in.

AUNT ARCTIC SAYS

Choose a color:

3. **Create Password:**

Enter Password

Confirm Password

4. **Parent's Email Address:**

Enter parent's email address

☐ I agree to the PRIVACY POLICY and TERMS OF USE

☐ I agree to the CLUB PENGUIN RULES

Next ➡

Using Your Toolbar

Once you log in, it's helpful to know how to use your toolbar.

 Click here to see a list of prewritten comments. Click on any of the comments and the words will appear in a speech bubble over your head. It's a quick way to say "hi" or ask a question, such as "Where did you find that pin?"

 Click here for a list of emotes—little icons that show how you're feeling without using words.

 Click here for a list of motions you can make: dance, wave, or sit.

 Click on the snowball to throw a snowball. A target will appear on your screen after you click. Move the circle to the place you want your snowball to land. Then click.

Use this bar to type in your own messages if you are not in Ultimate Safe Chat. As you type, you can click on any of the words and your penguin can begin chatting with other penguins right away.

If you are a member, click on the badge to bring your Player Card up on the screen.

 If you are not a member, you can click on the star instead of the badge to bring up your Player Card.

 Click on the orange penguin to see a list of your friends. You can click on a friend's name at any time to see their Player Card.

 Click on the house to enter your igloo.

Click on the gear to get to your account settings. You can mute your music and view your ignore list. You can also find out how old your penguin is.

Do More with a Membership

Club Penguin is free to play, but membership offers more opportunities to explore, create, and customize—plus access to exclusive items, parties, and game levels! A parent or guardian can sign you up for a membership and pay a monthly fee.

Create More: Purchase clothing, decorate your igloo, and discover special actions that your penguin can do.

Explore More: Access more levels in games and explore new areas first.

Play More: Adopt as many as twenty puffles.

Access More: Get backstage passes at parties.

Celebrate More: Attend members-only events.

You're In! What Now?

Explore: Waddle around by using your mouse to move your penguin. Follow the paths to different areas of the island.

Use the Map: Click on the [MAP] on the lower left of your screen. Then click on where you want to go.

Find Your Igloo: Click on the [home icon] in the toolbar if you want to chill out in your igloo.

Find Out the Latest: Get the news by reading *The Club Penguin Times*. Click on the [NEWS] on the top left of your screen.

Take a Tour: Ask a Tour Guide to show you around so you don't have to explore on your own.

Town Center

First stop: the Town Center! In this busy place, you can make some new buddies by joining in on the action. Penguins come to chat, dance, have snowball fights, and just hang out.

Head into the Coffee Shop for a steaming mug of cocoa, bust a move at the Night Club, or shop for an outfit that shows off your personality in the Gift Shop. There's something for every penguin in the Town Center!

Kick Back in the Coffee Shop

These comfy red couches are the perfect place to curl up with a hot beverage and *The Club Penguin Times*. You can also chat with buddies while a server wearing a green apron offers you a drink. Or get a job at the Coffee Shop and become a server yourself.

If you're looking to earn extra coins, waddle over to the bags of java and play *Bean Counters*. If you're the type of penguin who is interested in the arts, head upstairs to the Book Room.

HINT

If you like the service your penguin waiter has given you, don't forget to leave a tip. Press the *E* and *M* keys on your keyboard at the same time and a coin emote will appear.

If you have a green apron, you can earn the Coffee Server Stamp. It can sometimes be found for sale in the Gift Shop. You can perform the pouring coffee action by wearing only the apron and pressing *D* to dance. Serve five coffees while using the ☕ emote to earn the Stamp.

AUNT ARCTIC SAYS

Earn some coins at the Coffee Shop by waddling over to the bags of java behind the counter to play *Bean Counters*. You'll be paid in coins to catch the bags of coffee beans as they are tossed from the back of the van. Once you've caught the bags, you have to stack them on the platform.

Catch and Carry: You begin each game with three chances to empty all five trucks. Move your mouse left and right to get under each bag and catch it. Drop off the bags on the platform by clicking your mouse. Don't carry more than five bags at a time, or you will collapse under the weight!

Earn Coins: Earn points for every bag you catch and drop on the platform. Every time you empty a truck, the points you earn for catching and dropping off bags will increase. If you empty all five trucks, you will earn bonus coins.

Avoid Falling Objects: If you get hit by an anvil, a fish, or a flowerpot, you will lose one of your chances to complete the game. If you get hit by an object three times, the game ends, but you get to keep the coins you've already earned.

GAME TIP

The falling objects are easier to avoid once you know where they fall. The anvil always falls close to the truck, the fish falls close to the platform or in the middle, and the flowerpot falls in the middle. If you get hit, don't worry—catch the shining star with a penguin inside to earn an extra turn.

JAVA

PENGUIN ART

N TO
AY
CALA

HINT

With your mouse, scroll over the books on the bookshelf carefully. You might find some hidden items!

Book Room

If you like to read, you'll love the Book Room! Check out the bookcase and find books about Club Penguin history, stories written by the Writing Contest winners, and Captain Rockhopper's very own journal. Be sure to admire the artwork on the wall, done by your fellow penguins. Find out how to submit your own artwork. Maybe one day you'll see your own masterpiece hanging there.

In the Book Room, penguins can also challenge each other in a game of *Mancala*.

Mancala

Mancala is a fun game, but it can be hard to learn at first. Read the basics here and then play a few games. You'll be surprised how quickly you get the hang of it. Just ask Rockhopper. It's one of his favorite games.

Find a Friend: Waddle up to a table and join a penguin waiting to get started, or ask a friend to join you.

Capture Stones: The object of this game is to collect as many stones as possible before your opponent. At each turn, a player takes a group of stones from one hole on his or her side of the board. The player then drops each stone one by one into the holes around the board. This includes his or her mancala (the bigger hole at the end of your board), but not the opponent's mancala. The winner is the player with the most stones in his or her mancala and on his or her side of the board when the opponent has no more stones.

Develop a Strategy: This takes some practice. Put your mouse over a hole to find out the number of stones in it. Try to plan ahead. If the last stone you drop in a turn lands in your mancala, you will get a free turn.

If All Else Fails, Click: When it's your turn, click on one of the piles of stones on your side. You'll see how the stones move around on the board.

I enjoy playing multiplayer games with my friends, but it can be frustrating when all the game tables are taken. However, you don't have to sit and twiddle your flippers while you wait! Cheer on the players by becoming a spectator. All you have to do is click on the game table while a game is in progress. You'll be watching the action in no time!

AUNT ARCTIC SAYS

GAME TIP

Try reading the instructions on the wall before you play. That will help, but the best way to get good at *Mancala* is to play a few games.

Art Gallery

Ever wonder how to get your art into the Book Room's Art Gallery? Wonder no more—here are some top tips.

Keep on Trying: There's not enough room to show all the great art that gets sent to the gallery. So if yours doesn't get displayed, don't be discouraged. Send it again or draw another picture.

Practice, Practice, Practice: Like anything you do, the more you do it, the better you get. Why not set a daily art challenge for yourself?

Avoid Words: It's hard to read writing on a piece of artwork. For best results, just send in the image alone.

Be Original: Stand out from the crowd by sending in your unique ideas. Draw your own version of puffles or penguins. You can even design your own clothes and items for that personal touch.

I love to see the creative work that penguins send into the gallery. Did you know that you receive a rare postcard whenever your art is displayed?

AUNT ARCTIC SAYS

Bust a Move at the Night Club

As soon as you hear the thumping bass pounding out of the speakers in the Night Club, you'll want to dance! Grab a set of headphones and mix beats at the DJ3K machine or get funky on the dance floor.

If you want to put your dancing skills to the test, you can dance solo or challenge other penguins at the *Dance Contest*. If the music gets too loud, you can head upstairs to the Arcade. But before you do, run your mouse over the green puffle on the speaker. That little green guy can really groove!

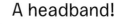

Meet Cadence

Occupation: Cadence grooves to her own beat! She's a DJ, musician, artist, dancer, choreographer, and all-around awesome penguin. You'll often find her at the Night Club mixing tracks for penguins to bust a move to. She's one of Club Penguin's best dancers, and break dancing is her specialty.

Bet You Didn't Know: Cadence has a purple puffle named Lolz.

Fashionista Alert: Cadence is one hip and confident penguin who always sports the coolest looks. She loves to wear bright colors. But her favorite fashion accessory is her smile!

Nicknames: Fans of Cadence have been known to call her "Dance Machine" and "Mix Master." In fact, she even calls herself that sometimes. She's also known as "DJ K-Dance."

What She Can't Live Without: Music!

Art Lover: Cadence is interested in all of the arts, not just music and dancing. She's just as happy checking out penguins' art in the Book Room or taking in a show at the Stage as she is dancing in the Night Club.

Favorite Items: Her green headphones and boom box.

Favorite Type of Music: Funk, techno, classical, trance—Cadence can mix and groove to anything with a solid bass line and a beat.

Unlock a hidden level in *Dance Contest*! When you are choosing your difficulty level, click on Cadence. She'll ask you if you'd like to try expert mode. But she'll also warn you that it's very difficult. She's not kidding. It truly is for expert dancers only!

How do you make a bandstand?

You take away their chairs!

If you're like Cadence and love to boogie, try playing *Dance Contest*—and earn some coins while you're at it! At the Night Club, head over to the table under the poster that says "Dance Contest Sign Up" to begin dancing. You'll need to hit the arrows on your keyboard to make your penguin dance.

Match the Arrows: When the colored arrows rise up to the gray arrows at the top left of your screen, press the matching arrow key on your keyboard. If two arrows rise at the same time, you need to push both buttons on your keyboard. Hold down the key during long arrows for a score bonus.

Combos: Hit a bunch of arrows in a row correctly to get a combo bonus and do some cool dance moves!

Timing Is Everything: To score more points, you've got to hit the correct arrow key on your keyboard at just the right moment, when the colored arrows match up with the gray ones.

Just Starting Out?: Choose the "How to Play" option to get a dance lesson from Cadence. Then start on the "Easy" setting, and work your way up to "Hard."

Go Solo or Share the Floor: If you choose "New Game," Cadence will clear the dance floor for you so you can dance by yourself. Or you can groove with other penguins when you select "Multiplayer." If you choose to boogie by yourself, you'll also get to select which songs you dance to.

Playing *DJ3K* is a chance to mix, match, and scratch your way to a musical masterpiece. Waddle over to the DJ table in the Night Club and click on the speakers on the left side of the table to start making your own music. The longer you play, the more coins you'll earn.

Mix It Up: There is no right way or wrong way to play *DJ3K*. All you need to do is play around with the two turntables, the cassette players, and the other equipment to lay down your perfect track.

Hone Your DJ Skills: Click on the different buttons and levers to discover what sounds they create. You'll hear sirens, whistles, car horns, and more! Play around to figure out what combination gets your penguin dancing, and you'll earn extra coins.

Record and Save: At any time during *DJ3K*, you can click the "Record" button to make a copy of your song. When you are finished, click "Stop." Listen to the song you just created. If you like it, you can save your song and give it a name. It will automatically be added to your igloo. If you don't like it, click on "Cancel" and you can start recording all over again.

Igloo Replay: You can play your song in your igloo. Click on the ⌂, then on the ▭ and go to "My Saved Mixes" to find your song.

GAME TIP

If you click on the "Game Upgrades" icon in the Night Club, you'll get the option to buy records you can use while playing *DJ3K*.

000 Hit the Ta

Gamers' Delight in the Arcade

There's even more to do at the Night Club! Head up to
the second floor to find the Arcade. You can chill out in
old-school style with classic arcade games like *Thin Ice*,
Astro-Barrier, and *Bits and Bolts*. Or kick back and watch
the dancers below. There's a window in the floor that lets
you keep an eye on all the action on the dance floor. And
you can even grab a beverage out of the vending machine
while you relax.

HINT

Certain items can help you dance in different
ways. Look for the Penguins at Work section
in the Gift Shop's Penguin Style catalog or for
rare items at special events like Music Jam.
When you've bought an item, make sure you are
wearing only that item and press [D] to dance.
You'll be grooving to a different beat!

THIN ICE

A black puffle that has turned fiery red is the star of this game. Use your keyboard arrows to complete the maze by moving the puffle over blocks of ice. The more ice blocks you melt, the more coins you'll earn.

Move and Melt: At each level there is a different maze, and there are nineteen mazes in all. The object is to move the puffle from the starting point to the end of the maze, which is a red block. As you pass over blocks of ice in the maze, you'll melt them. You can't pass over these blocks more than once or you'll sink and have to start the level over again.

Earn Coins: You can take the easiest path each time to finish the maze, but you'll earn more coins if you melt as many blocks of ice as you can.

Special Tiles: Each maze is more difficult than the next. In some mazes, the red tile will be blocked by a locked door and you'll have to find the key before you can exit. As you progress, you'll find light blue, dark blue, and green tiles that all do different things. Move carefully to find out what they are!

THIN ICE

ASTRO-BARRIER

HINT

There are coins hidden in the levels of *Thin Ice*. If you complete a level by melting all the ice tiles, a bag of coins will appear in the maze in your next level. Be sure to grab it as you go!

GAME TIP

On Level Nineteen there is a false wall in the top right corner of the maze. Move through the false wall until you reach the block with the circle inside it. When you melt this block, an extra bag of coins will appear for every level you have completed. Be sure to grab each bag.

45

In this game, you'll get to blast away at objects as they fall from space. *Astro-Barrier* can be found in the Arcade next to *Thin Ice*.

Move and Shoot: Press the left and right arrow keys to move your ship. Press the space bar to shoot the moving objects overhead.

Make Every Shot Count: If you run out of bullets on a level, you will lose a turn. If you keep shooting without aiming, your game will be over pretty quickly.

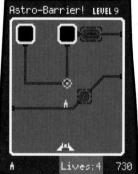

Plan Your Shots: If you hit a target, it becomes a wall, making it harder for you to shoot the other targets. One strategy is to hit the targets on top first, then the ones underneath.

Score Points: You earn ten points for each target you hit, and bonus points each time you clear a level.

You can skip ahead to more challenging levels in *Astro-Barrier*. When you get to the Start menu, don't click on "Start." Instead, press the number one on your keyboard to go to Level Ten, or the number two to go to Level Twenty, or the number three to go to Level Thirty.

There are also secret levels in this game. After Level Ten, an instruction box will appear on the screen. Don't hit "Enter" to keep playing. Instead, wait about twenty-five seconds. A blue ship will appear. Shoot it, and you will be taken to the secret levels where you can earn extra points.

ASTRO-BARRIER

Two plus two equals four, but it can also equal a piece of a robot in the fast-paced factory game *Bits & Bolts*. It takes some quick thinking to match the bolts to the display number, especially as the game goes on (and gets faster)!

Connect the Bolts: Click on the bolts to equal the number shown. For example, if the number is five, you must click on either a five-bolt piece, a three-bolt piece and a two-bolt piece, two two-bolt pieces and one single bolt, or five single bolts.

Click Quickly: When you correctly click on the number of bolts that matches the target number, you will clear those blocks from the screen. Try to clear as many blocks as quickly as you can.

As the game goes on, the pace gets more frantic. Stay calm and concentrate to make it to the next level.

GAME TIP

Build a Robot: To earn more coins, look at the right of the screen. You'll see "Bot Parts" with the word "Only" and a picture of a bolt piece. If you use only the bolt piece shown to make up the target number, you will create a piece of a robot.

Bolt Overload: If you make a mistake and click on a bolt combination that goes over your target number, more bolts will fall down. You need to clear all the blocks on the screen to advance to the next level. If you let the bolts reach the top of the screen, it's game over!

Blast Balls: Special blocks with "+" and "-" signs will fall. Click on these blast balls to remove several bolts from the screen at once. But don't use them too early in the game. Save them until you really need them.

Buy Yourself a Gift at the Gift Shop

Tired of your old color? Want to rock a flaming red Mohawk? Or are you looking for the perfect outfit to fit the latest Club Penguin party theme? You'll find colors, wigs, costumes, and much more at the Gift Shop.

Located next to the Night Club, the Gift Shop is the place where penguins can buy clothes and other items from the monthly Penguin Style catalog. A new catalog is released the first Thursday of every month. Use the coins you have earned from playing games to buy things from the catalog.

Discover Your Penguin Style

Here are some of the things you can find in the Penguin Style catalog to update your look.

Tired of Your Old Color? Pick a new one!

Create Your T-Shirt: Design your own wearable work of art.

Get the Latest Looks: New and seasonal items are featured in every catalog.

Penguins at Work: Each catalog features a different uniform. You'll find clothing items for jobs such as lifeguard, coffee server, firefighter, construction worker, and more.

Clearance Items: Don't miss your last chance to buy the items featured on the Clearance pages. They won't be seen for a while.

Player Card Backgrounds: Change the look of your Player Card with a new background.

Choose a Flag: Put a country flag on your Player Card to show where you're from or where you'd love to visit.

Secret items are hidden inside each new Penguin Style catalog. They are not always easy to find, but I think searching for them is just as much fun as finding them. Move your mouse over the images on the pages and watch for the mouse pointer to change to a hand. When it does, click—you'll be able to see and buy a secret item.

AUNT ARCTIC SAYS

The Underground

Let's go underneath the busy streets of Club Penguin to discover exciting areas just waiting to be explored. Beneath all the snow and ice, you'll find the Cave Mine, the Hidden Lake, the Boiler Room, the Underground Pool, and the Mine.

You can find the entrance to these rooms aboveground at the Mine Shack. We'll begin our tour in the Boiler Room.

Click here to go to the Night Club.

Find and read old editions of *The Club Penguin Times* here.

Secret passageways are so mysterious, aren't they? You can find one of the secret entrances to the Underground in the Plaza. Click on the manhole cover in front of the Pet Shop to start exploring.

AUNT ARCTIC SAYS

I was going to say a penguin with a sunburn!

Take a Swim in the Underground Pool

Walk through the green door in the Boiler Room and you'll be in the Underground Pool—a cool underwater hangout. You'll see penguins getting their flippers wet in the pool. Feel free to take a dip. You can dive in as you are, but you'll notice that some penguins dress up for a swim in bathing suits, scuba gear, mermaid costumes, or life jackets and snorkels.

Don't feel like getting wet? Hang out on the side of the pool and watch the strange creatures that swim past the windows. Or climb into the lifeguard chair and watch over your fellow penguins as they splash around.

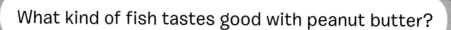

What kind of fish tastes good with peanut butter?

After a long day of writing, I love to relax with a refreshing dip in the pool. You, too, can swim in the pool, if you've got the right clothing items. Wear the water wings, inflatable duck, or lifeguard uniform and dance, and you will swim when you press .

AUNT ARCTIC SAYS

If you use the secret entrance to get to the pool, you will earn the Underground Stamp.

HINT

Jellyfish!

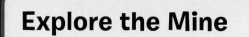

Explore the Mine

Waddle through the dark tunnel to the right side of the pool to find the Mine. Don't let the spooky shadows scare you! The Mine is a dark and quiet place, but adventure is only steps away. Go on a wild ride by playing *Cart Surfer* or put your bravery to the test by helping puffles in peril at *Puffle Rescue*.

In the past, the Mine has had several rockslides. Penguins put on hard hats to help dig out. The big, open space of this room has made it perfect for parties. During the Medieval Party, a fire-breathing dragon took up residence here. A banana peel replaced the mine carts during an April Fool's Party. Make sure to visit the Mine during a party. You never know what you'll find!

I admit, I'm a Club Penguin trivia buff. But there are some things about the island even I don't know. For instance, no one is sure exactly who built the Mine Shack or for what reason. I don't mind not knowing. Mysteries are just as fun as trivia!

AUNT ARCTIC SAYS

Hop on board a mine cart for a wild ride! In this fast-paced game you will travel at high speeds through the Mine. To begin, enter the Mine by walking underground through the Cave or aboveground into the Mine Shack. Then walk into the mining carts.

Away You Go! You don't have much time to think with this game–as soon as it starts, your cart is off for a wild ride! Hold on tight and try to make it through without tipping over.

Tricky Turns: When you see a turn coming up, lean into it or you'll crash! To lean left, hold down the left arrow key, and to lean right, hold down the right arrow key. Watch out: If you lean for too long you will wipe out. You only get three carts. Once you're out, the game is over.

Mining for Tricks: The secret to scoring big at *Cart Surfer* is to do tricks. Press the space bar to jump and press the up and down arrows to try different moves. But don't try to do a stunt while turning or you will crash! The more tricks you do, the more coins you'll earn.

Cart Surfer is one exciting ride. I've got to hold on to my hat when I play it! I love to try new tricks, but sometimes learning them can be a bit tricky. The best way to figure out how to do different tricks is to try different combinations with your arrow keys and space bar. Here are a few tricks to get you started:

360° Turn: Hit [SPACE] and then [←] or [→].

Backflip: Press [↓] and then [SPACE].

Handstand: Press [↑] twice.

Rail Run: Hit [↓] twice.

AUNT ARCTIC SAYS

The Mine Shack

At the Mine Shack, you'll find the entrance to the Mine as well as the Community Garden and the Recycling Plant. Here you can help water the garden by throwing snowballs into the green bucket. Thanks to all the penguins who have helped at the garden, the tree that was planted here after Earth Day has grown very large. In fact, it's taller than the Mine Shack now!

The green building is the Recycling Plant. Go inside and throw your trash into the Recycletron 3000 to turn it into something new. To do this, simply throw a snowball into the machine. These snowballs will appear as trash that can be recycled, such as old pizza boxes, barrels, empty hot-sauce bottles, and more. Try it and see what you can recycle.

What did the tree wear to the pool party?

Swimming trunks!

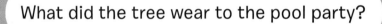

Penguins are always asking me about the mysterious statue of a polar bear that turned up in the Mine Shack one day. To learn more about this bear, stop by the Everyday Phoning Facility in the Ski Village. If you pass the test, you'll be let in on a lot of Club Penguin classified information.

AUNT ARCTIC SAYS

Some puffles have gotten themselves into serious trouble and it's up to you to save them! The blue puffles are stranded on ice, surrounded by hungry sharks. The pink puffles are trapped on rocks, high inside a cave. The black puffles are underwater, with some electrifying shocktopi between them and safety. Go to the Mine and look for the sign for *Puffle Rescue* over the bulletin board to start playing.

Pick Your Puffle: There are three different versions of the game: blue puffle, pink puffle, and black puffle.

To the Rescue! Use the arrow keys to move. The object of the game is to find the puffles and bring them back to the start square.

Watch Out! In the blue and pink versions, be careful not to fall off the ice blocks or the mine carts and boxes. In the black puffle version, make sure you don't run out of air. You will lose a life.

Avoid: Sharks, snowballs, and shocktopi. Look out for cracked ice and rickety boxes. If you stand on them too long, they will break and you will fall.

PUFFLE RESCUE

GAME TIP

In the first level of the black *Puffle Rescue,* you can find the key to the Hidden Room.

Timing Is Everything: Watch and wait before moving. Sometimes you need to time it just right to avoid losing a life.

Extra Turns: For every level you complete, you earn an extra turn. You begin the game with three turns but can gain up to five more.

Don't have a hard hat?
You'll find one here.

Dig for Treasure in the Cave Mine

Grab a hard hat and start digging! You can find buried coins in the Cave Mine if you dig. You'll need a shovel or a hard hat to do so. Make sure you are only wearing a hard hat or holding the shovel, nothing else. Then dance. If you don't find any coins, try digging in a new spot.

Throw snowballs in here to turn the lights on.

Click here to go to the Hidden Lake.

DID YOU KNOW?

The Cave Mine was first discovered during the Cave Expedition of 2010.

The Mystery of the Hidden Lake

Check out all the treasure that can be found in the Hidden Lake. No one knows where the shiny gold and gems came from. One thing we do know: They make the Lake, with its sparkling waves and cascading waterfalls, even more beautiful.

You can get to the Hidden Lake from the Cave Mine or from the Forest.

The Underwater Room:
Swim under the sea with the fishes in the colorful Underwater Room. To find this hidden spot, you must play the black *Puffle Rescue*  mini-game and find the key. In the first level, save the puffle but don't go back to the start square. Wait for the squid and follow it to the Hidden Room. Once you have the key, you'll be able to visit the room anytime you want, without having to play *Puffle Rescue*. You'll be able to walk through the locked door at the Hidden Lake.

The Plaza

PET SHOP

PUFFLES

LIVE ACTION

The Plaza has it all. Looking for an adorable puffle to call your own? You'll find it right here at the Pet Shop. Want to be the star of a play? Or just kick back, relax, and watch a show? You can be a performer or a member of the audience at the Stage. And when you get hungry, grab a slice at the Pizza Parlor.

With so much to do here, it's no wonder that penguins flock to the Plaza every day.

Take a quiz to find the perfect puffle for you and adopt puffles here.

Each puffle has a unique personality. Learn about them all here.

I simply adore my puffles! They are so much fun to play with. But they do need taking care of. Puffles must be kept happy and healthy with regular food, sleep, baths, and exercise. If you don't take good care of your puffles, they will leave your igloo and return to the wild.

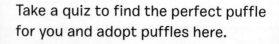

AUNT ARCTIC SAYS

Explore underground caves with your puffle when you play *Pufflescape*.

Blast off on an adventure in *Puffle Launch*.

When you play *Puffle Roundup*, you can earn coins by helping herd puffles back into their pen.

Puffle Paradise in the Pet Shop

At the Pet Shop, you can adopt a puffle. Puffles are small, furry creatures with big personalities. There are ten types of puffles, and each color puffle is different. They all have one thing in common: They are fun to take care of and make great pets!

Buy toys, houses, food, and furniture for your puffles here.

The Great Puffle Discovery

Before puffles were discovered, penguins were puffleless! In November 2005, all that changed when small, furry creatures were spotted near the Snow Forts. Scientists found out they were animals that lived in the wilds of Club Penguin. They also learned they were very friendly.

A contest was held to name the creatures. Penguins submitted over one thousand ideas! In the end, the name "Puffles" won.

After that, penguins were able to adopt puffles and keep them in their igloos as pets. The first puffle colors discovered were blue, pink, green, and black. Eventually, purple, red, yellow, white, orange, and brown puffles were found.

I ♥ MY

How to Pick Your Puffle

To adopt a puffle, waddle over to the puffles in the Pet Shop and click on them. You can take a quiz to find out which puffle is most like you. When you are finished with the quiz, you can adopt the puffle that you have the most in common with. Or you can click on a different puffle and adopt that one. Some puffles are adventurous, some are creative, others are silly. Read all about the different puffle personalities in the Puffle Handbook. The choice of which puffle to adopt is up to you!

It costs 800 coins to adopt a puffle. Everyone can adopt up to two puffles—red or blue. Members can adopt up to twenty puffles in ten different colors.

Puffle Personalities

Every puffle is different. You can learn a lot about your puffle by playing with it and feeding it.

Black Puffle

Although mostly quiet, the sudden, fiery outbursts of black puffles show the intense side of their personality.

Blue Puffle

These loyal and content puffles are known for their awesome teamwork.

Brown Puffle

Supersmart and inventive, brown puffles have superior machine-building skills.

Green Puffle

Playful and funny, green puffles love to laugh and will have you cracking up, too.

Orange Puffle

You'll never be bored with a curious and zany orange puffle in your igloo.

Pink Puffle

Pink puffles love to exercise and swim.

Purple Puffle

Stylish purple puffles are fabulous dancers.

Red Puffle

Adventurous red puffles were first discovered on Rockhopper Island.

White Puffle

They may be smaller than all other puffles, but white puffles are very powerful.

Yellow Puffle

Artistic yellow puffles are always creating something new.

Pet Papers

Food, toys, and items you can use to care for your puffle will be displayed here. Drag the item to your puffle to use it.

Read about your puffle's personality and print out a copy of its adoption certificate here. You can also return your pet to the wild. If you do this, your puffle will leave your igloo. Only do this if you're really sure, because it can't be undone!

Caring for Your Puffle

After you adopt a puffle in the Pet Shop, your new pet will be waiting for you inside your igloo. Go there to start taking care of your new puffle pal. Click on your puffle to care for, play with, and feed it.

Puffles love to play! Click here to play with your pet. Drag a toy to them. They'll only play with a toy they like.

Click here to dress your puffle in different hats.

You can wash or brush your puffle when you click here.

You can give your puffle a nap when you click here.

To feed your puffle, you'll need to buy food from the Puffle Catalog. Click on the bowl to see the different kinds of food you have. Pick the treat you'd like to give your pet and drag it to them.

DID YOU KNOW?
Your puffle will let you know when it is happy, sad, tired, or hungry.

PETS

Shopping for Your Puffle

In the Pet Shop, click on the  to shop for your pet. You can also access the catalog from your igloo. Here are some things you can buy:

Food

Buy food and water dishes to add to your igloo. You can also stock up on snacks like carrots, bubble gum, cookies, pizza, and Puffle O's for your puffles.

Toys

These items will inspire your puffle to play! When you buy one of these toys, it will be added to your igloo storage. (To learn more about decorating your igloo, turn to page 210.) Put it in your igloo, sit back, and watch the fun.

Super Toys

Each puffle color will only play with its own toys. Buy a special toy for your puffle here. When you click on your puffle and then click on the 🌐 you can drag the toy to your puffle.

Houses

Give your puffles a comfy spot to escape the hustle and bustle of your igloo. Houses are also added to your igloo storage.

Bedzzz

Give your pet a soft area to snooze. Like houses and regular toys, beds will be added to your igloo storage.

Explore Club Penguin with Your Puffle

Click on your puffle. Then click on the 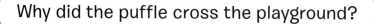. You'll find the 🐛. Drag it to your puffle to take it for a walk. You can only walk one puffle at a time. Click on the map and pick a place to take your puffle for a stroll. Try using the dance motion and see what your puffle does!

Why did the puffle cross the playground?

To get to the other slide!

Play Games with Your Puffle

Did you know that you can take some puffles into mini-games with you? If you do, it may help you earn more coins! Take your puffle for a walk. Then go to one of the mini-games. Simply play the game like you'd usually do, but this time you'll have a puffle along to help! Here is a list of puffles and the mini-games they can play:

 Red puffles can play *Catchin' Waves*.

 Purple puffles can play *Dance Contest*.

 Yellow puffles can play *DJ3K*.

 Pink puffles can play *Aqua Grabber*.

 Black puffles can play *Cart Surfer*.

Green puffles can play *Jet Pack Adventure*.

 Any puffle you own can play *Puffle Launch* and *Pufflescape* with you. You don't even have to walk them. Simply go to the game and you'll find them waiting there for you.

Meet PH

Hi there!

PH is an all-around puffle expert. If you need to know anything about puffles, she's the one to talk to. PH also works for the EPF as an Elite Puffle Trainer.

Proudest Moment: After the Puffle Party of 2011, PH came up with a new design for the Pet Shop. It changed how penguins and puffles interacted, and gave puffles the perfect place to express themselves even more.

Favorite Snack: PH loves Puffle O'berries so much, she eats them right off the bush!

She's Most at Home: Anywhere puffles can be found. She can chill out in her igloo with her puffles, or wander off into the wilds of Club Penguin for days to observe puffle behavior.

Favorite Possession: You'll never see PH without the whistle she wears around her neck. She uses it to train puffles.

Bet You Didn't Know: It was PH who left the trail of notes during the Wilderness Expedition. Doing so helped penguins discover the brown puffle.

PUFFLE ROUNDUP

Get a job at the Pet Shop and earn some coins by helping herd the puffles back into their pen.

Move Your Mouse: Use it to herd as many puffles as you can into the brown pen.

Scoring: Your score will be based on the number of puffles you can catch within the shortest amount of time.

Puffle Wrangling: Puffles can be pretty tricky. Some will run away before you can get them into their pen. Try not to steer the puffle off the screen.

It's Not Over Until: A round ends when all the puffles are herded into their pen or time runs out. After each round, you can choose to keep playing or end the game and collect your coins.

Send your pet puffle flying through the skies in this exciting game. Click on the big red cannon in the Pet Shop to get started. At the beginning of the game, you'll see all the puffles you own. Choose one and get ready to blast off! If you don't own any puffles, you'll be able to take a red puffle into the game.

Fly Through the Sky: Press the space bar to launch your puffle from the cannon. Use the left and right arrow keys to steer.

Collect Puffle O's: Try to get your puffle to pick up as many Puffle O's as possible. This will help you earn pieces of the cannon you are building as you play. You can check your progress with the bar that is located on the bottom of the start page of the game. But watch out for the cranky crab—he is after the Puffle O's, too!

Stay Airborne: Your puffle needs to jump from cannon to cannon, or use objects like balloons to bounce off, to stay in the air. If your puffle falls, you will go back to the beginning and have to start over. On some levels your progress will be saved at a checkpoint and you can start from there.

Aim for the Fiery Puffle O: To end each round, you must guide your puffle past the obstacles and get it through the Fiery Puffle O.

Unlock Levels: There are three levels of play in Puffle Launch: Blue Sky, Soda Sunset, and Box Dimension. There are twelve rounds in each level. You need to complete a round before the next one will unlock. You must complete all rounds in a level to move on to the next level. Your game progress will be saved, so you can pick up where you left off the next time you play.

Know Your Cannons: Different colored cannons work differently.

Green Cannon: Can shoot left, right, up, and down.

Blue Cannon: Fires the moment your puffle touches it.

Purple Cannon: Can rotate in a 360-degree circle.

Red Cannon: Spins in a circle—click to blast off!

Checkered Yellow Cannon: Acts as a mini checkpoint.

Pufflescape

Explore underground caves with your pet puffle in this fun puzzle game. Click on the plastic puffle ball in the Pet Shop to start your journey. At the beginning of the game, you'll see all the puffles you own. Choose one and get ready to roll! If you don't own any puffles, you'll be able to take a white puffle into the game.

Explore the Depths: Use the left and right arrow keys to steer your puffle through underground caves. Try to move certain objects by dragging and rotating them using your mouse. Move the objects to create useful ramps and bridges for your puffle.

Unlock Levels: You can play three different levels in *Pufflescape*: The Entrance, The Depths, and The Legend. Grab the key in each level to unlock the door and complete a round. There are eight rounds in The Entrance and The Depths levels. The Legend has seven rounds—the last round has three parts for your puffle to complete.

Collect Puffle O'berries: You can unlock hints for each level by collecting at least one Puffle O'berry. The hints will help you collect the Puffle O'berry bunch. Grab the bunch, and your puffle will unlock the Extreme mode for that level!

Enjoy the Show at the Stage

Grab some buddies and bring the latest play to life at the Stage!

Be a leading penguin by taking a role in the latest Stage production. The set will change every time a new play is performed.

Not interested in acting? Sit back and watch the performance in these comfy seats.

Click the buttons and pull the levers to create special effects.

SWITCHBOX 300

It's no secret how penguins get to these stylish seats. Just click on the balcony from the stage and you'll waddle right up.

Open the script and click on the lines to read them onstage.

Penguins can buy costumes and special backgrounds here.

CHECK IT OUT

You don't have to stick to the script. Use the provided script for inspiration. Then get creative and come up with your own ideas!

COSTUMES

SCRIPT

COSTUME TRUNK

How to Put on a Play

Here's what you need to know to put on a spectacular show:

Cast and Crew Needed: Unless your play is a one-penguin show, you'll need some help. Head to the Stage and ask the other penguins already there to pitch in. Or send a postcard inviting your buddies to the Stage. To send a postcard, click on the  at the top of your screen, then on "New Message" to choose a postcard and mail it to a friend. Once you are all there, decide which roles everyone will take.

Be a Director: The director is in charge of the production and can help decide who should do which jobs. If you're a good leader, go to the Costume Trunk. Buy a director's cap, put it on, and help guide the actors. You can let them know when to begin and where to stand. (You'll even find lines in the script to give you ideas of what you can say.)

Be an Actor: Once you know what role you are playing, click on the script. You don't have to memorize any lines! Simply click on the lines of your character. Use the *Costume Trunk* to outfit yourself for the role.

Be a Stagehand: Put the *special* into the special effects of your play by being a stagehand. Waddle over to the Switchbox 3000. Click the buttons and pull the levers to control the sets, turn on spotlights, and create special effects.

Be an Usher: Escort penguins to their seats before the big performance and show them how to get into the balcony.

Be in the Orchestra: If you own an instrument, get together with other musicians to provide live music for the show. Set up in the black area in front of the Stage. It's called the Orchestra Pit.

Be a Ticket Taker: Walk into the ticket booth in the front of the theater. When a penguin approaches the booth, ask, "Would you like a ticket?" Or just greet them with a smile. Soon you'll have curious penguins lining up to check out your play!

Be in the Audience: Sit back and be entertained! Let other penguins know if you like the show by using your emotes.

Encore, Encore!

Here's a list of plays that have appeared on the Stage. Which was your favorite?

Once upon a time, this fabulous fantasy transformed the Stage into a fairy-tale forest.

The show must go on, but how can it when a ghost is causing trouble and the leading lady refuses to perform?

When a laser shrinks an absentminded professor to the size of a bug, he gets lost in a giant garden!

Chester gets his flippers on a time machine and steps into it. The rest is *prehistory*.

Can an explorer survive breaking bridges, snowball attacks, and crocodiles to discover the mysterious golden puffle statue?

Leaving no fish unturned, Detective Jacque Hammer is on the case to find Ruby's missing valuable gem.

Monkey King searches for the Phoenix Queen's treasure, meeting many interesting characters along the way!

Blast off in search of alien life and adventure on the SS *Astro-Barrier* spaceship.

A giant squid attacks, and it's Shadow Guy and Gamma Gal to the rescue!

Cheer on your favorite mascot at the mascot tryouts and during an epic dodgeball game.

To fish or not to fish, that is the question. A group of penguins sets out to meet a rare fish.

Daisy and Fearless Fiesel journey into the mystical depths of the ocean to discover a lost underwater city.

More Things to Do at the Stage

Penguins have thought up lots of creative ways to use the Stage that have nothing to do with putting on a play! Here are just some of the ways the Stage has been used.

- Play hide-and-seek here. The different play sets let you hide underwater and even in outer space!

- Hold a costume contest or a fashion show. Penguin judges use emotes to show if they like your outfit.

- If you are in a band, have a concert here.

- Form an improv acting troop. Improv stands for improvisation. That's when you make things up on the spot. Have audience members shout out suggestions. You and your buddies can act them out.

What other ideas can you come up with?

When the Stage was first built, a yellow puffle was hiding in the balcony. Today, the yellow puffle always makes an appearance during the show. Sometimes you really have to look or play around with the Switchbox 3000 to spot it!

Grab a Bite at the Pizza Parlor

The Pizza Parlor is always hopping with hungry penguins!

Earn coins by making pizza in the kitchen when you play *Pizzatron 3000*.

There's a lot of work to do in the Pizza Parlor. You can be the manager or take a job as a waiter, cashier, or pizza chef.

HINT
Want to toss pizza dough like a pro? Buy a chef's hat when it is on sale in the clothing catalog. Click on the dance action on your toolbar to start tossing pizza dough.

FISH DISH

Are you in a band? Grab your instruments and hold a show on the stage here or play a solo on the piano.

If you're a hungry customer, take a seat. Use the 🍕 when you are ready to eat. A waiter or chef should stop by and take your order.

Hungry penguins from all over flock to the Pizza Parlor to eat pizzas. You can earn lots of coins if your pizza-making skills are fast enough to feed them!

Order Up: A pizza crust will slide by you on the conveyor belt. It's up to you to add the toppings to get the order right. Look at the order screen in the top right corner to see what kind of pizza you have to make.

The Perfect Pizza: Drag and drop items onto the pizza crust. Your customers will ask for pizza sauce, hot sauce, cheese, seaweed, shrimp, fish, squid, or a combination of these toppings.

Oops! If you make a mistake on a pizza, it won't sell, but you'll get the chance to make it again. If you make five mistakes, penguins will stop buying your pizza and it's game over!

Earn Extra Coins: After you make five perfect pizzas in a row, you start to earn tips from happy customers. Your first tip is ten coins. If you keep making pizzas without making mistakes, you'll get more tips.

Fast Flippers: The pizzas get more complicated the further you get in the game—and the conveyor belt speeds up! Pay attention but move quickly to get all your orders done right.

Before you start making pizzas, look for the red lever on the conveyor belt. Click on it and then press start. You'll be making pizzas topped with chocolate sauce, icing, sprinkles, and chocolate chips!

GAME TIP

The Forest

and the Cove

Penguins love to head out into the great outdoors. With all that space, there's no better place to throw a party! Come with me and I'll show you two perfect party spots: the Forest and the Cove.

Imagine It All in the Forest

The Forest is a big space with plenty of pine trees to hide behind. It's no wonder that penguins love to play all kinds of games here. From hide-and-seek to tag to games penguins make up themselves, the Forest is a great place to get creative and have a good time.

Amazing Transformations

The Forest can look very different during Club Penguin parties. Here are just a few ways it has changed in the past:

- Trick or treat? The friendly Forest becomes a spooky place every year during the Halloween Party, with paths leading to a Haunted House and the Dark Chamber.

- Penguins could explore the bamboo forest during the *Card-Jitsu* Party in November 2011.

- A Forest of fun! Puffle games, prizes, and more fill this space during the Fair.

- Adventure in the great outdoors awaits! Penguins camped out and explored the tree forts that were added to the Forest during the Adventure Parties.

- Penguins thought they had to stand on their heads to make their way through the upside-down Forest during the 2008 April Fool's Day party.

Card-Jitsu Party

Island Adventure Party

Halloween Party

DARK CHAMBER

HAUNTED HOU

HINT

Try moving the big rock in the Forest. A secret entrance to the Hidden Lake is underneath!

Hang Ten in the Cove

Surf, hang around the campfire with your buddies, or take a swim at the Cove.

Gather your friends and tell stories around the campfire. You may see some penguins roasting marshmallows on sticks. The sticks were first given away at the Camp Penguin Party held in 2007.

Hop into the lifeguard chair to keep watch over the swimmers in the Cove. Look through the binoculars and watch for any dangers that could be lurking in the sea. Lifeguard shirts are available from time to time in the Penguin Style catalog.

Click on the blue note attached to the pink surfboard. You'll find two surfboards you can buy and carry with you into *Catchin' Waves*: the Daisy and the Flame. A third board can be found if you click on the word *waves*. The silver board will unlock. Hold on to it tightly—the silver board makes you go faster!

Go to the Surf Hut to check out the amazing waves in the Cove. You can play *Catchin' Waves* here.

CATCHIN' WAVES

Cowabunga! Head over to the Surf Hut to perform totally tubular tricks. It takes practice to become a good surfer, so don't give up.

You can expect to wipe out a few times before you get the hang of it.

Getting Started: Choose from Surf Lesson, Freestyle, Competition, and Survival. If it's your first time, take the Surf Lesson to get warmed up. Practice in Freestyle mode before you move on to Competition and Survival.

Hanging Ten: Use your mouse to steer up and down, lean forward and back, and keep your balance.

Tubular Tricks: Use your keyboard to perform tricks. You can press either the W, A, S, or D keys or the arrow keys while you are surfing. Try pressing different combinations of keys to perform advanced tricks. "Shoot the tube" by surfing very close to the curl of the wave. Don't get too close to the wave or you'll end up wiping out!

Basic Moves:

| Wave | W or ↑ | Handstand | A or ← |
| Sit | S or ↓ | Dance | D or → |

Advanced Moves:

The Lazy Wave
(Wave + Sit)
[W] + [S] or [↑] + [↓]

Coastal Kick
(Handstand + Dance)
[A] + [D] or [←] + [→]

The Backstand
(Sit + Handstand)
[S] + [A] or [↓] + [←]

Surf Fever
(Dance + Wave)
[D] + [W] or [←] + [↑]

Ice Breaker
(Handstand + Wave)
[A] + [W] or [←] + [↑]

Blender
(Sit + Dance)
[S] + [D] or [↓] + [→]

Earn Coins: The more tricks you do, the more coins you will earn!

The Forts

and Stadium

wednesday

Some of the best spots on Club Penguin for outdoor activities are the Snow Forts and the Stadium. Find some friends and play a game of soccer or ice hockey. Chill in the bleachers and watch a game. Or start a snowball fight! Whether you're into sports or just like to play in the snow, you're sure to find some fun in these areas.

Have a Ball at the Snow Forts

In the mood for a snowball fight? Then head to the Snow Forts and start throwing snowballs. Other penguins will usually join in the fun. To throw a snowball, click on the ⦿ on your toolbar. A target will appear on the screen. Move the target to the place you want your snowball to land, and click. Watch your snowball fly!

If you want to practice your aim, you can throw snowballs at the target on the Clock Tower. Gary the Gadget Guy built the snowball-powered clock. He designed it so that when a penguin aimed a snowball at the target attached to the clock, the inner gears would wind up.

The clock is set to PST—Penguin Standard Time. PST might be different from the time on your computer, but every penguin on the island will see the same time on the clock. That makes it easier to meet up with your buddies.

To throw snowballs more quickly, use a keyboard shortcut. Put your cursor over the spot you'd like to hit and press the  **T** key on your keyboard. (Make sure your cursor is not inside the chat bar, or this will not work.) A target will appear. Click to throw a snowball, and then keep pressing **T** to throw a bunch of snowballs very fast. Start a snowball fight using this shortcut. It's a great way to meet new penguins, and it's a lot of fun!

AUNT ARCTIC SAYS

STADIUM

Help out as an announcer and give the play-by-play of the game.

PIZZA | SPORTS

Join in on the action and start a game.

Game Time at the Penguin Stadium

Sports fans love hanging out at the Stadium!

SNACKS

SPORTS

Grab a snack to munch on while watching the game.

Manage the equipment or sell tickets to games here.

Cheer on your favorite team from the bleachers.

Buy items for your igloo, sports gear, and clothing here.

FEE

PUFFLE

THE STAGE

SLED RAC

Snow and Sports

Suit Up

Before you start playing at the Stadium, you might want to suit up with some cool sports gear. You can find these items in the Snow and Sports catalog, which you can find in the Stadium. There are items in here that you won't find in the Penguin Style catalog. New items appear in each catalog, but don't worry if you don't see an item you need. Older items are brought back all the time, so keep checking.

Choose a Team: All sports jerseys, uniforms, and cheerleader outfits come in red, blue, green, and yellow. You and your friends can choose a team and dress in matching uniforms.

For the Fans: Not an athlete? Don't sweat it! You can sit back in the bleachers with oversize foam fingers in the color of your favorite team to cheer them on. Sports games need a referee, and you'll also find a referee jersey and whistle in the catalog.

A Sporty Igloo: Show off your love of sports in your igloo with items like weights, benches, gym mats, scoreboards, and more.

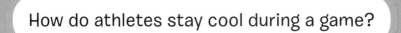

Ice Hockey and Soccer

Would you rather shoot a puck across an icy surface or dribble a ball on artificial turf? No matter which sport you want to play, these tips will help you start a game.

Suit Up: You can purchase uniforms and gear, such as a soccer jersey or a hockey stick, in the Snow and Sports catalog. You don't need these to play, but suiting up can help to psych you up!

Find Friends: Get the word out to your friends that you want to have a game. You might want to send a postcard to do this.

Divide into Teams: It helps if each team chooses a color so it's easier to see who's on your side when you pass the ball. If you don't have jerseys, you can change your penguin color.

Get the Ball or Puck in the Goal: Use your mouse to move your penguin toward the ball or puck. Push the puck into the goal. Choose one penguin from each team to protect your goal. Once a goal is made, the ball or puck will automatically appear in the center.

Keep Score: The team with the most goals at the end of the game wins. You can also just play for fun.

Form a team with at least five other penguins wearing the same color jersey to earn the Soccer Team Stamp.

GAME TIP

and the *Migrator*

"Look! The *Migrator* is coming!" excited penguins cry when they spot the pirate ship through the telescope on top of the Beacon. They know that when Captain Rockhopper comes to town, he always brings something exciting and new with him.

Even when the *Migrator* isn't around, the Beach and the Dock are fun places to hang out. Here you can get some sun on the Beach, listen to a band at the Lighthouse stage, go on a *Jet Pack Adventure*, or play *Hydro-Hopper* at the Dock.

Surprises at the Dock

When there's a party on Club Penguin, make sure to head to the Dock. There's almost always something exciting going on here. At the April Fool's Day Party in 2010, penguins could throw snowballs at a giant easel and watch them splatter into paint splotches. And at the Music Jam Party in 2011, the Dock featured a performance stage complete with a judges stand and a secret backstage area.

When it's not party time, penguins with a need for speed jump into the boat for a game of *Hydro-Hopper*. Or you can just hang out and catch some rays at this seaside spot.

What kind of vegetable do you never want in your boat?

A leek!

HYDRO-HOPPER

Grab a tube and hold on tight as a speedboat tows you over the ocean waves! You'll earn coins by jumping over anything in your way.

Choose Your Gear: You can play with a red inner tube, but if you click on the red note attached to the pink wakeboard you can buy a wakeboard to play with. Make sure you are holding it when you play the game, and you will earn more coins when you jump.

Avoid Sharks: . . . and other obstacles in the water. Use your mouse to move and left click to jump. If you hit something, you'll fall off the tube.

Buoy Bother: You can't jump over buoys—they are too tall. Avoid them instead.

Look for Life Preservers: Pick one up to earn an extra life.

Earn Extra Coins: Avoiding objects won't earn you any coins, but jumping over them will. And if you jump over two objects in a single jump you'll earn even more.

Hydro-Hopper was the very first mini-game on Club Penguin. Back then, it was called Ballistic Biscuit.

AUNT ARCTIC SAYS

Get Onstage at the Lighthouse

Every music fan should rock out at the Lighthouse! Grab an instrument such as a guitar, drum set, trombone, or tuba, and then dance. The sound of your instrument will join with those of other penguins to play a song.

The Lighthouse stage is also a great place to hold a talent show with your friends. You can also get behind the microphone and tell your favorite jokes.

During the Medieval Party, the Lighthouse sometimes gets transformed into a wizard's tower, complete with potions and books of magical spells.

CHECK IT OUT

Introducing . . . the Penguin Band!

You'll find lots of penguins playing music on the island, but there is only one official band—the Penguin Band! They appear at parties and never miss the Music Jam. If you are lucky enough to run into a band member backstage, you'll be rewarded with an autographed background.

Drummer G. Billy has also been known to play the harmonica.

Petey K may be a prankster, but he's got some serious accordion skills.

When the band first appeared in 2005, all of the members were blue! Then they showed up as a Hawaiian band, and then a country band. In 2011, they updated their style and added rock, alternative, and electronic music to their set.

Franky gives the band a techno twist with his electric keyboard.

Stompin' Bob keeps the beat with his bass guitar.

Look here and you might see a calm sea, storm clouds, the *Migrator*, or other surprises.
Turn the light on and off by flipping on this switch.
OFF

Get a Great View at the Beacon

At the top of the Lighthouse you'll find yourself on one of the highest points on all of Club Penguin. Play *Jet Pack Adventure* to soar over the island, or look through the telescope to see what's on the horizon.

The bright light guides Captain Rockhopper's ship safely to shore.

Who says penguins can't fly?

JET PACK ADVENTURE

Thanks to Gary the Gadget Guy, penguins are able to take to the skies in the high-flying game *Jet Pack Adventure*. Soar above the island, collecting coins along the way.

Watch Where You Fly: Use your arrow keys to control your jet pack. Try to fly into coins, fuel, and extra jet packs. Avoid obstacles such as coffee bags and anvils. Crashing into them will slow you down and eat up your fuel.

Safe Landing: The only safe areas to land are the designated landing pads at the end of each level.

Look Out Below! If you run out of jet packs, the game is over. You will use your parachute to glide to the ground somewhere on the island. If you finish the game, you'll end up on the landing pad in the Mine.

Fuel for Thought: Keep your eyes open for extra jet packs—if you catch one, you'll get an extra life in case you run out of fuel.

Try This Twist: If you complete the entire game without collecting a single coin, you will get a bonus of one thousand coins at the end!

Your green puffle can help you earn Stamps in this game. Get a Stamp when your puffle collects coins, a fuel can, or just plays the game with you.

The flag on a pirate ship is called the Jolly Roger. This one looks more like a Jolly Puffle!

Yarr is the first red puffle that Rockhopper discovered. The two have been friends ever since.

STORE

Climb down into the Hold, the area below decks to see what treasures Captain Rockhopper has brought with him.

Up here you can hang out with Yarr and shoot snowballs out of the cannon by clicking on it.

Click your arrow on the mast to visit the Crow's Nest.

Climb Aboard the *Migrator*!

When Captain Rockhopper lands on Club Penguin, he docks his ship, the *Migrator*, at the Beach. Rockhopper prefers traveling with only his trusty first mate, Yarr, but he allows penguins to visit his ship when he's docked.

Meet Rockhopper

Occupation: Pirate captain of the *Migrator*, the finest ship to ever sail the seven seas.

Where He Calls Home: This sailor may hail from Club Penguin, but his heart belongs to the sea.

Best Matey: His puffle, Yarr, a true-blue friend with bright red fur.

Most Memorable Discoveries:
- Discovering the red puffle.
- Landing on the shores of Rockhopper Island.

Favorite Drink: Why, that would be cream soda, of course!

Bet You Didn't Know: Captain Rockhopper built the *Migrator* with his own bare flippers.

I keep a record of all of me adventures in me journal. You can find them in the Book Room!

Meet Yarr

Occupation: As first mate of the *Migrator*, Yarr helps make sure the ship smoothly sails the seas.

Special Talent: This brave buccaneer has a gift for surfing the ocean waves.

Where You'll Find Him: When he's not hanging in the Crow's Nest and shooting snowballs out of the cannon, he's exploring Club Penguin with the captain.

Bet You Didn't Know: Yarr got his name because every time Captain Rockhopper called out, "Yarr!" he came running.

CHECK IT OUT

The *Migrator* will appear on the Club Penguin home page when the ship docks at the island. Move your mouse over the ship to see Yarr jump around in the Crow's Nest.

HINT

When Captain Rockhopper is visiting Club Penguin, the best places to look for him and Yarr are the *Migrator*, the Dock, the Iceberg, the Beach, and the Pizza Parlor. If you find him and ask him to be your buddy, he will give you a signed photo of himself.

Find Treasures Below Deck!

In the ship's Hold, Rockhopper sells some of the rare treasures he's found. He usually gives one item away for free! After browsing the Captain's bounty, head to the Captain's Quarters, where you'll find even more riches by playing *Treasure Hunt*.

Rockhopper's Treasure Trove: Captain Rockhopper brings all kinds of special items with him:

 Clothing, such as the Tricorn Hat.

 Furniture items, such as the Barrel Chair.

 Backgrounds, such as the Island Grove Background.

 Fun stuff, such as the Stuffed Parrot.

Treasure Hunt

Captain Rockhopper finds so many amazing treasures on his travels that he created this game so he can share them with other penguins. The key to success is cooperation.

Dig It: The game takes place in a box of sand. You and your friend take turns digging up rows of sand in the box. If you dig in the right spot, you will uncover treasure!

Coins and Jewels: Be on the lookout for these treasures while digging. Red rubies are worth twenty-five coins, a gold coin is worth one, and the rare green emerald is worth one hundred coins. To earn your reward, you'll have to uncover each coin or jewel completely.

Work Together: If your friend digs up a piece of a jewel, make sure to dig next to that piece on your turn. It's the only way to completely uncover the treasure. You and your friend will get six turns each, so choose your moves carefully!

GAME TIP

Look for a sparkle underneath the sand. It's a clue that there may be a jewel or coin buried there.

My good friend Captain Rockhopper and I both enjoy making lists. When you are in his quarters, be sure to check out his notice board. You'll see some interesting photos, plus you can learn what he's up to by reading his to-do list.

AUNT ARCTIC SAYS

CHECK IT OUT

Be sure to play this game in December if you can. The sand sometimes changes to snow, and you'll find candy canes, peppermint candies, and ornaments buried there.

How Adventurous Are You?

Do you have what it takes to sail the seas with Captain Rockhopper? Take this quiz to find out!

1. Which of these is your dream vacation?
   a. Playing video games for a whole week.
   b. Going to the beach.
   c. Climbing to the top of Mount Everest.

2. You won a contest! You get to travel around the world, but you have to leave right away. Do you:
   a. Turn down the prize. You'd rather stay at home.
   b. Ask if you can leave after you have a chance to pack.
   c. Head out right away. This is the trip of a lifetime!

3. You're following a treasure map and it leads you to an underwater cave guarded by an octopus. Do you:
   a. Give up. You're not going in there!
   b. Find an octopus expert to bring with you.
   c. Keep going. No eight-legged critter is going to stand between you and your treasure!

4. You're at a play and the lead actor can't perform. You happen to know all the words by heart. Do you:
   a. Go home and watch a movie.
   b. Go and see another play.
   c. Jump onstage and take the part yourself. The show must go on!

5. You're at a restaurant and the cook wants you to try a brand-new dish. It doesn't look like anything you've ever seen before. Do you:
   a. Order a burger instead.
   b. Ask to read the recipe.
   c. Take a big bite. It could be delicious!

Check Your Adventure Score:

If you answered **mostly *a*'s**, you are not very adventurous. You'd rather stay in the Book Room and read Captain Rockhopper's journal than go exploring with him.

If you answered **mostly *b*'s**, you are adventurous but you're cautious, too. You like to know exactly what you're getting into when you jump in. You might enjoy a short trip on the *Migrator*, but sailing into uncharted waters might be too much for you.

If you answered **mostly *c*'s**, then you are just as adventurous as Captain Rockhopper! You're not afraid to jump right into any new or exciting situation. You'd make a great first mate on the *Migrator*.

The Ski Village

There's always a lot going on in the Ski Village. You can race down the Ski Hill, go *Ice Fishing*, learn how to be a Tour Guide like me, or chill out in the Ski Lodge.

And what's with that Everyday Phoning Facility? It's nothing special . . . or is it?

Join the Rescue Squad!

A penguin is stranded on top of the Ski Hill! A fierce storm is whipping across the island. Who do you call?

The Club Penguin Rescue Squad, of course! Rescue Squad members are ready to spring into action if a disaster strikes. You can become a member if you have the uniform. Check the Penguin Style catalog's "Penguins at Work" page and buy it when you see it. Then join the effort to help keep Club Penguin safe.

CHECK IT OUT

Form a squad with your friends. Arrange to meet at a specific time and location and patrol the area, looking for penguins who need help.

150

If you are wearing only the Rescue Squad uniform and helmet, press [W] to wave. Your penguin will hold up the Rescue Squad sign, notifying those around you that you are there to help.

The strong yet stylish helmet protects the Rescue Squad member in dangerous situations.

Insulated material keeps Rescue Squad members warm in the most frozen conditions.

Every sled run has at least one ice patch on it that will help you move faster if you slide over it. In the Bunny Hill, the ice patch is in the middle of the race. Look for the patch on the Express Run near the bottom. The patch on Penguin Run is about a third of the way down. And Ridge Run has four ice patches: two near the top, one in the middle, and one three-quarters of the way down.

AUNT ARCTIC SAYS

RIDGE RUN

PENGUIN RUN

Hold on to your snow hat! This run is supersteep and loaded with obstacles.

The perfect run for penguins with a need for speed.

Get Ready to Race at the Ski Hill

If you're revved up for some winter sports action, hop on the Ski Lift to be carried to the top of the Ski Hill. This spot has one of the best views on Club Penguin. But the main reason penguins come here is to have sled races against one another. You can't race alone, so if the Ski Hill is empty, send a Sled Race postcard to a buddy who's online at the same time as you. Ask them to join you for a race.

On New Year's Eve, Club Penguin celebrates with an amazing fireworks show that lights up the sky. The Ski Hill and the Iceberg are the best places to watch the spectacle.

CHECK IT OUT

Can you say *wipeout*? This tricky run is full of traps to trip you up.

Need to practice? Do the bunny hop right over this easy hill!

BUNNY HILL

EXPRESS

Sled Racing

Whether you're in the mood for an easy glide or feel like sliding at superspeed, there's a sled race for you!

Find a Race: Walk to one of the sled runs. The Bunny Hill is the easiest run and the best way to learn the game. Ridge Run is the most difficult. The race can't begin until enough penguins join in, but if you wait a little bit you'll usually find a racing partner.

Don't Wipe Out: Use your arrow keys to move left and right as you speed down the hill. Avoid obstacles such as a log or tree branch. If you hit one, you will wipe out. But you'll quickly get back on your snow tube and continue racing.

Finish First: The race ends when all penguins cross the finish line. You will earn coins depending on how you place.

When you get to the end of a race, look for the two blue penguins at the bottom of the hill. They love to cheer for all of the racers!

AUNT ARCTIC SAYS

GAME TIP

Each time you jump over an obstacle, move back to the center of the run. From that position, it's much easier to work out what your next move will be.

This legendary big fish can be caught while playing *Ice Fishing*.

MULLET

Every half hour the cuckoo clock chimes and a yellow bird pops out and yells, "Cuckoo!" The bird's name is Fred.

Warm Up in the Ski Lodge

After a day of playing in the cold and snow, you might want to relax in front of a warm fire. You'll find one inside the Ski Lodge. This rustic log cabin is where penguins come to hang out. There are comfy couches to lounge on, and some interesting wall hangings to check out, including a moose head and a cuckoo clock. You can play *Find Four* or *Ice Fishing* here, too.

This slow-paced game is a nice way to relax and earn coins at the same time. To play, head to the door marked "Gone Fishing" at the back of the Ski Lodge.

Catch Fish! You must have a worm on the end of your hook to catch a fish. Move your mouse up and down to raise and lower your hook. When you see a fish, lower your hook to catch it. Raise your hook above the ice and click your mouse to release the fish.

Avoid Obstacles: Barrels and boots can kick fish off your line. Jellyfish, sharks, and crabs will cost you a worm if they touch your line.

Watch Your Worms: If you lose a worm, raise your hook above water level and click on the can of worms to get a new one. Once you lose all three of your worms, the game is over. Before that happens, try to catch a can of worms to get an extra life.

Collect Your Coins: At the end of the game, you will receive one coin for every fish you catch. If you catch the extra-big Mullet at the end, you will get an extra one thousand coins.

GAME TIP

Getting shocked by a jellyfish can make you lose the game if it happens enough, but if you get shocked three times and still finish the game you will earn a stamp! You can also earn stamps by feeding a fish to a shark and catching several fish in a row without making a mistake.

Many penguins are puzzled about how to capture the Mullet at the end of the game. The secret to catching him is to catch the yellow Fluffy fish and leave it dangling on your hook. You can use this fish for bait. Mullets love them! If you succeed, you'll earn an extra one thousand coins.

AUNT ARCTIC SAYS

Hide Out in the Lodge Attic

Looking for a quiet spot to chat with a friend? This is the place. You can play a game of *Find Four* up here, too. Challenge your friends in a tournament to determine the ultimate champ.

Many attics have hidden secrets. You can find unusual surprises in the Lodge Attic, too. After the big snowstorm in year two, the extra snow was stored here and then used for the Festival of Snow. During the Medieval Party in year four, the room became the top floor of a pink castle. Sunlight streamed through stained-glass windows, blue water bubbled from indoor fountains, and the old rocking horse was transformed into a white stallion. What will find its way into the Lodge Attic next?

Some penguins have pointed out to me that the rocking horse in the Lodge Attic is much taller than any penguin. They're right! I even tried to climb on it myself, but didn't succeed. I've been asking around to find out who made it, but no one seems to be sure.

AUNT ARCTIC SAYS

What kind of horse likes loud music?

A *rocking* horse, of course!

Find Four

If you're good at problem-solving, *Find Four* is the game for you. Once you learn the rules, it's easy to master.

Find a Partner: Walk to a game table to challenge a partner who's sitting there, or wait for someone to challenge you.

Get Four in a Row: The object of the game is to be the first player to stack four round game pieces of the same color in a row. You can stack them either up and down, across, or diagonally. Your name will be highlighted when it is your turn to play. When it's your turn, click on the slot that you would like to drop your piece in. You and your opponent will take turns until one of you gets four pieces in a row.

Find Four is a game of strategy, not speed! Before you make a move, think about how you can win *and* block another player from winning at the same time.

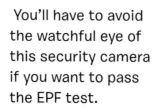

You'll have to avoid the watchful eye of this security camera if you want to pass the EPF test.

Top Secret: Inside the EPF

The Everyday Phoning Facility located in the Ski Village may look ordinary, but it's the entrance to one of Club Penguin's biggest secrets: the Elite Penguin Force.

Inside this building you can take a test to become an EPF agent. Once you pass the test, an elevator will take you to the EPF Command Room. But think carefully before you accept this position: EPF agents keep a watchful eye over Club Penguin, facing peril and danger at every turn.

If you click on the lights from left to right, the lights in the room will dim. Click on the farthest light on the right to turn the lights back on.

Defeat enemy robots in the *System Defender* game.

If you sit in one of the chairs, the EPF logo will appear on the big screen. If there is a penguin in each chair, the screen will reveal secret information.

TUBE

M SCANNER

ELITE P

EXIT

EPF

FIELD

Enter here to be taken to the Virtual Reality Room. In here you can train by carrying out past missions from the old Penguin Secret Agency. For fun, click on the Hologram Controls to see what different secret-agent headquarters looked like in the past.

Sometimes the Director sends all agents on a new Field-Op. Click here to find out what to do.

FORCE

The EPF Command Room

This room is the hub of all EPF activity. Once you become an agent you'll get a spy phone, which is always on the bottom left of your screen. Click on the phone's yellow button to come directly to the Command Room.

Strengthen Your Skills

Agents can specialize in skills they are best at to become a stronger part of an EPF squad. There are four different agent classes to choose from. You can choose to master one, or strengthen your abilities in all four. Using the medals you earn through Field-Ops, you will be able to get elite gear and advance in the different classes.

Comm Class

Instructor: Rookie

What You'll Learn: How to intercept intelligence, jam signals, maintain communication with Command, and give and receive orders. Comm Agents help keep the team connected in dangerous situations.

Gear: Comm Helmet, Sat-Pack, Comm Gear, Comm Boots

Advantage: Penguins who like leadership and use information to solve problems make great Comm Agents.

Tactical Class

Instructor: Jet-Pack Guy

What You'll Learn: Combat strategy; snowball-throwing skills

Gear: Alpha Headset, Delta Headset, H2O Pack, Range Finder, Tactical Gear, Tactical Boots

Advantage: If you like action and solving problems head-on, then you're a natural addition to the Tactical Team.

Tech Class

Instructor: Gary

What You'll Learn: How to hack into enemy systems and shut them down; how to manipulate electronics and computers to the team's advantage

Gear: Optic Headset, Tech Coat, Tech Satchel, Tech-book 3000

Advantage: If you like cutting-edge technology and solving problems using your intellect, the Tech Class is for you.

Stealth Class

Instructor: Dot

What You'll Learn: How to slip past security cameras, firewalls, sentries, motion detectors, and other barriers without being noticed

Gear: Dark Vision Goggles, Blue Power Cell, Canister Camouflage, Sneak-ers

Advantage: Penguins who are secretive and solve problems by patiently waiting for the solution to reveal itself are built for Stealth.

Dot

Occupation: As the disguise specialist for the EPF, she creates advanced disguises for agents.

Where You May Have Seen Her: Saving former PSA agents from a popcorn explosion in the "Veggie Villain" mission.

Defining Moment of Awesome: She created the Klutzy disguise, which allowed agents to infiltrate Herbert's lair.

Rookie

Occupation: As a new Penguin Secret Agent, Rookie made a lot of mistakes. But now he leads the Comm Team for the EPF.

Where You May Have Seen Him: He accidentally allows the bots to escape in the *System Defender* game.

Notable Quote: "Go, rubber ducky! The fate of the island rests in you!"

Jet-Pack Guy

Occupation: This sharp-dressed penguin leads the EPF's Tactical Team.

Where You May Have Seen Him: In "G's Secret Mission," he is the agent who rescues you after you are stranded in the wilderness.

He's Unique Because: He's the only penguin who can wear a secret-agent tie and a jet pack at the same time. His sunglasses are custom, too.

Who Is the Director?

We'd love to tell you, but nobody knows. Not even Agent G, the Director's most trusted agent, knows his or her true identity.

Meet Gary

Greetings and salutations!

Occupation: Gary the Gadget Guy, also known as Agent G, is the highest-ranking official in the EPF, and answers only to the mysterious Director. He sends agents on Field-Ops and guides them in missions. He's also the most well-known agent, because he's Club Penguin's resident inventor.

What You Might Be Surprised to Learn: Every Halloween, Gary watches the spooky "Night of the Living Sled" series. "I enjoy the part where they mistake the normal sled for the Living Sled," Gary says. "That's a distinctly hilarious scene."

Greatest Moment: During the Festival of Flight, Gary lifted the entire island into the sky!

Is It Possible to Meet Gary?: Gary is always busy creating new things, and he doesn't enjoy big crowds. He's more interested in tinkering with tools than going to the latest parties. But sometimes he does venture out. He's been spotted at the Penguin Play Awards, the Festival of Flight, and, of course, at some Halloween parties. If you meet him and friend him you can get a special background with his signature on it.

Favorite Food: Fish Dish pizza. (It's why he invented the Pizzatron 3000.)

SOLAR POWERED OXYGEN ENRICHER

Gary's Inventions

Just about every cool gadget you see on Club Penguin has sprung from the mind of one genius: Gary. When Gary invents something new, you can usually read about it in *The Club Penguin Times*. Here are some of his most memorable creations:

Mini-Games: *Jet Pack Adventure, Pizzatron 3000, Aqua Grabber, DJ3K*

Party Items: Monster Maker 3000, Island Lifter 3000, Breeze Maker 3000

PSA Mission Items: spy phone, Crab Translator 3000, life preserver shooter

EPF Items: EPF spy phone, Spy Camera 3000, Solar-Powered Flashlight

Other Memorable Inventions: snowball-powered clock, box portals

These Are No Ordinary Puffles!

A group of Elite Puffles has been recruited by the EPF. They are specially trained by PH, the Elite Puffle Trainer, to help with secret missions.

 Bouncer: This blue puffle is an expert snowball thrower.

 Blast: This energetic red puffle can shoot himself out of a cannon.

 Flare: This black puffle can burst into flames, which enables him to weld objects.

 Loop: This cheerful pink puffle can lasso moving objects.

 Pop: This bubble-blowing purple puffle can lift heavy items.

 Flit: This green puffle is a fast flyer.

 Chirp: This yellow puffle can play the flute at pitches so high, they can shatter ice.

 Chill: When this white puffle blows on something with his icy breath, it freezes.

Meet PH

Occupation: This Elite Puffle Trainer is the world's foremost expert on puffles.

Where You Might Have Seen Her: During the Wilderness Expedition in 2011, PH left the trail of notes that led to the discovery of the brown puffle.

Defining Moment of Awesome: PH worked with puffles to invent the game *Puffle Launch* as a new way for pets to play and exercise.

You can get Stamps when you earn five, ten, twenty-five, and fifty EPF medals.

How to Succeed at Field-Ops

Sometimes, Gary asks all EPF agents to perform a Field-Ops task. If you succeed, you will earn a medal that you can use to purchase elite spy gear. Here are some tips for mastering Field-Ops:

Get Your Instructions: When you hear your spy phone ring, click on it. It's probably Gary. He will tell you to report to the Command Room for a new Field-Ops mission. Transport there using your phone and then waddle over to the Field-Ops console. Click on the screen to get your mission.

Start Your Search: The first part of your task will be to find the location of your mission. Sometimes there is a clue in Gary's instructions. For example, if he says a machine on the island needs to be fixed, transport around and walk up to all the machines. When you hear a beeping sound, you will know you are in the right spot.

Work with Other Agents: Sometimes it's difficult to find the location. Go back to the Command Room. If you are able to chat, ask the other agents there if they know where to find the Field-Ops mission. A helpful agent will send you in the right direction.

Master the Test: Once you are in the right spot, the Field-Ops task will appear on your screen. Read the instructions and give the test a try. Don't worry if you don't get it right away—keep trying. It doesn't matter how many times you fail. Just make sure you master it before the next Field-Ops mission is posted, because you won't have another chance after that.

Earn Medals: Each time you successfully complete a Field-Ops mission, you will earn one medal. Click on the shield symbol on your spy phone and you will see how many medals you have earned. You can use those medals to get Elite Gear.

FORCE

Bring on the Bad Guys

EPF agents work tirelessly to stop the dastardly deeds of these villains. They want to make sure that Club Penguin is no fun for anyone!

Herbert P. Bear

Occupation: Aspiring Supervillain

Where You May Have Seen Him: There is a statue of Herbert outside the Mine Shack. He's also behind just about every disaster to hit Club Penguin. The popcorn explosion that destroyed the old PSA was Herbert's work.

Quirks: Even though he's a polar bear, Herbert hates the cold. He's also a vegetarian!

Inventions: The Underground Driller, the Electromagnet 1000, and the Ultimate Proto-Bot 10000

Klutzy

Occupation: Herbert P. Bear's Partner in Crime

Where You May Have Seen Him: In the third level of *System Defender*, Klutzy sends the Pro-bots to attack the EPF mainframe. He's also the crab you must track down in the Questions for a Crab mission.

Bet You Didn't Know: Klutzy saved Herbert from drowning when he first arrived on the island.

Quote: "Click click clickey click!"

Ultimate Proto-Bot 10000

Occupation: The leader of the Test Bots, he is programmed to destroy the EPF.

Where You May Have Seen Him: The final level of *System Defender* is the most difficult—thanks to Ultimate Proto-Bot and his powerful Bot army.

History: When Gary's Test Bots went bad, they created Ultimate Proto-Bot. Then Herbert P. Bear rebuilt him, making him bigger and better.

In this game of speed and strategy, you will defend the EPF's system mainframe from invading Bots.

Take the Tutorial: The first time you play, click on Tutorial to get a lesson from Gary. When you think you've got the game down, you can try any of the six advanced game levels. Each time, you'll face a different villain.

It's All About Energy: As Gary will tell you, your job is to build cannons to destroy the enemy Bots as they enter the EPF system. You need energy to build cannons. Red cannons use fifty energy, Yellow use one hundred and twenty-five energy, and Purple use two hundred energy. You gain energy every time you destroy a Bot.

Place Your Cannons Carefully: Before the Bots attack, look to see where they enter and where the system mainframe is. When you start out, don't put all your cannons in one spot. It's a good idea to guard the entrance, the mainframe, and any turns in the grid first.

Pick Up Batteries and Gears: Sometimes Bots that have been destroyed will drop batteries. Click on them to receive extra energy. Bigger Bots drop gears, which you can use to give your cannons extra power. Click on a dropped gear and drag it to the cannon you want to upgrade. But do it fast, because invading Bots will quickly destroy a gear.

Protect the Mainframe: Your object is to protect the mainframe at all costs. Every time an invading Bot hits it, the mainframe loses power. You will earn coins for every Bot you hit.

Pay attention to the EPF agents at the bottom of your screen. They will give you hints about which cannons you need.

GAME TIP

The Iceberg

What's so exciting about a huge frozen chunk of ice? Just ask the penguins who have made this one of the most popular places on Club Penguin. Head to the Iceberg and you're bound to find penguins hanging out or even having a party. You can also play *Aqua Grabber* here.

Gary the Gadget Guy invented the Aqua Grabber, a magnificent mini-sub.

HINT

You can't walk to the Iceberg. To get there, click on the map on your screen. Look for the Iceberg floating in the upper right-hand corner and click on it. You might be surprised by what's happening there!

Throwing a party at the Iceberg is a wonderful way
to meet new friends—and you can earn a Stamp,
too! If you are wearing a hard hat and drill the
Iceberg in a group of thirty or more penguins, you'll
get the Stamp. You can send a postcard to your
buddies inviting them to join you at the Iceberg,
or go into town or another crowded place and
announce your party there.

AUNT ARCTIC SAYS

Party at the Iceberg

Rumors have been swirling around Club Penguin for a long time that it's possible to tip the Iceberg. So penguins hold Iceberg parties, trying to get it to tip. There are many ways to take part in one of these parties.

Dance: Some penguins think that if enough penguins dance at the same time, the motion will tip the Iceberg.

Drill: You need the construction or miner's helmet to use a jackhammer. Head to the Cave Mine to pick up your free construction helmet. Wear the helmet and nothing else. Then dance and drill away!

Follow the Crowd: Join a group of penguins all standing on one side of the Iceberg to see if it will tip.

Chant: Start a rousing chant of "Drill! Drill! Drill!" or "Tip the Iceberg!" to get other penguins moving. Another popular chant is "Dance or drill, just don't stand still!"

Explore the depths of the ocean in a mini-sub as you hunt for treasure.

Choose Your Adventure: You can explore the Clam Waters or the Soda Seas. In each level you'll have three objectives: Find the Main Treasure, the Rare Treasure, and the Secret Treasure.

Move Around: Use the arrow keys to move up, down, left, and right. Press the space bar to operate the grabber's claw and pick up treasures. If an item is too big to fit in the Aqua Grabber, bring it back up to the net and use the space bar again to drop it in.

Grab the Goods: In the Clam Waters, grab pearls from the small clams when they open their shells. The Secret Treasure is a black pearl hidden in one of the clams. The Rare Treasure is a Giant Pearl inside a giant clam. In the Soda Seas, you'll be picking up cream-soda barrels. The Main Treasure is an Amethyst that you'll find inside a cave, and the Rare Treasure is an Emerald.

Get Some Air: Look for large air bubbles you can move over to fill up with extra oxygen. You can also get air by going above the surface of the water on the top of your screen or inside caves.

After playing *Aqua Grabber* many times, I've discovered some useful tricks that can help you succeed. For example, did you know that you can use your claw to push yourself up from the ocean floor? If you time it right, you can grab an item and give yourself a boost at the same time.

AUNT ARCTIC SAYS

The Dojo courtyard is a peaceful place. But inside, penguins can challenge themselves. Sensei built this beautiful building so aspiring ninjas could train in the ancient art of *Card-Jitsu*.

The Dojo is surrounded by three elements: water, fire, and snow. Water flows from the waterfall, fire burns deep inside the volcano, and snow covers the mountainsides.

Train Inside the Dojo

If you want to learn the ancient art of *Card-Jitsu*, you can practice in the training room. Penguins face each other to train and earn their belts. The ultimate prize is a black belt, and the honor of becoming a fully trained ninja.

Earn a white belt first and then work your way up to a black belt.

HINT

You can earn belts by playing on the practice mats or competing with other ninjas. You'll have to win multiple times to move on to the next belt. It may sound like a lot of work, but that's the whole point of ninja training—to slowly build up your skills until you become a master.

Want to talk to Sensei? Click on him to learn how to play *Card-Jitsu*. Sensei will set you up in matches with other penguins so you can earn your belts. You can battle Sensei at any time, but you won't have a chance to beat him until you've earned your black belt.

The mist flowing from the pot changes to reflect the three elements of *Card-Jitsu*: water, snow, and fire.

Click on the cards to see how far you've progressed in your quest to become a ninja.

You can practice *Card-Jitsu* with a partner on one of these mats. However, you'll earn belts faster if you ask Sensei to match you with an opponent.

Meet Sensei

Sensei's long, white beard is a symbol of the wisdom and secrets he has learned over many years of training. Luckily, he is more than happy to give advice to penguins who want to become ninjas.

> Every journey begins with a single step.

Occupation: Sensei built the Dojo. He trains penguins in the art of *Card-Jitsu*. To master *Card-Jitsu*, you must first defeat Sensei.

Why He May Surprise You: Sensei may look like a calm, peaceful penguin on the outside, but his skills make him a powerful *Card-Jitsu* competitor.

Memorable Moment: Penguins were excited when a fiery volcano awakened on the snowy island. Sensei tamed the volcano with a mysterious amulet. Then he showed other ninjas how to forge these amulets from gold and a mysterious black gem. The Amulet allows ninjas to play *Card-Jitsu Fire* and *Card-Jitsu Water*.

Favorite Word: *Patience*. Many students get frustrated when they can't get a black belt or ninja suit right away. Sensei advises them to keep training, and the rewards will come.

Favorite Things to Eat: Sensei loves to eat sushi, and a nice hot cup of tea always helps him think.

To master this game, you must understand the elements: water, snow, and fire.

Know the Elements: Think of *Card-Jitsu* as a game of rock-paper-scissors, but with cards. Water douses fire, fire melts snow, and snow freezes water. You and your opponent will each throw a card. The dominant element wins the hand. So, if you throw a fire card and your opponent throws snow, you win the hand. The winning card will appear on the screen above your player.

Numbers Count: If both players throw the same element, the highest number wins. So, if you throw a three snow card but your opponent throws a five snow card, your opponent wins the hand.

Collect Colors: To win *Card-Jitsu*, you need to win at least three rounds. You can win by having one card of each element, but each card must be a different color. Or, you can have three cards of the same element as long as they are all different colors.

Use Logic: Try throwing out cards with the highest number value first. As you learn the game, you can use logic to anticipate your opponent's moves. Let's say your opponent has earned one yellow fire card and one green water card. They need a snow card to win. Since you know that fire melts snow, you can throw a fire card to stop them from winning.

Know Your Power Cards: When certain cards are played, they'll change the rules for the next hand. The border of these cards will glow when they appear on your screen. Run your cursor over the card to see how the rules will change. If your opponent plays a special card and wins the hand, look for the symbol on top of your screen that will show you the rule change.

Boost Your Deck with Power Cards

Any ninja-in-training can master the elements with the cards that Sensei gives you. It just takes time and practice. But there is a way to speed up your training—it's what Sensei calls "The Fast Path."

To take The Fast Path, you'll need to use the ancient Power Cards. There are a few Power Cards in your starter deck, but you can get more by purchasing the *Card-Jitsu* Trading Card Game in stores. Type in the code that comes with the cards, and the cards will appear in your deck the next time you play.

Power Cards have high numbers, which means they can help you defeat your opponent more easily. But they also have special instructions that can change what happens on the next move. Even if you don't have Power Cards, it's good to know how they work in case your opponent uses them.

Here are a few examples:

SENSEI
Snow, Purple
When you play this card, your opponent must discard one water card.

FIREFIGHTER
Water, Yellow
When this card is played, be careful how you play the next turn. The card with the *lowest* value will win instead of the card with the highest value.

MIGHTY PLUNGER
Fire, Red
When you play this card, whichever card you play on your next turn will gain two points.

Throw a snowball at a gong and see what happens!

Journey to the Ninja Hideout

Once you have practiced some *Card-Jitsu* at the Dojo, find your way to the Ninja Hideout. Here you can choose to play *Card-Jitsu*, *Card-Jitsu Fire*, or *Card-Jitsu Water*.

Inside, you can buy ninja gear and begin the next phase of your journey: the journey to master the three elements.

ing Flippers
- Emporium -

Step into Flying Flippers Emporium and purchase special gear from the Martial Artworks catalog.

You need an Amulet to continue your journey by following the paths of water, snow, and fire here.

Penguins can buy a complete ninja outfit in the catalog. Combine the ninja outfit, your ninja mask, and the Cloud Wave Bracers to perform this amazing ninja skill: If you're wearing all three things and wave, your penguin will vanish into a shadowy form. The effect stops once you begin walking.

DID YOU KNOW?

Mastering the Elements

Beyond the Hidden Doors

In the Ninja Hideout you'll see three tablets, each with an element symbol on it. If you click on a tablet, a hidden door will appear. Walk through the door to enter the Fire Dojo or the Water Dojo.

Earn a Suit

You can train in each element to earn a Fire Suit or a Water Suit. You'll find practice mats in each Dojo, but the only way to earn your suit is to approach Sensei. Each suit has four pieces, so you'll earn one piece at a time.

Pick Your Path

You can take any of the ninja journeys in any order. You don't have to complete one to begin another!

Challenge Sensei

To become a true Fire Ninja or Water Ninja, you must defeat Sensei after you earn each suit. He will give you a gem to add to your Amulet.

Once you earn your Fire or Water Suit, you gain the power to change the weather! Meet up with many other ninjas, wear your complete suits, and press ⬚ to perform the dance action together. Then watch the sky for fiery reds, watery blues, and shadowy grays to appear!

GAMETIP

Penguins with a bold style who are not afraid to take chances can master the element of fire. In this game you can test your abilities against as many as three other ninjas.

Be Prepared: Once you have received an Amulet from Sensei, enter the Fire Dojo and talk to Sensei. He will give you a Fire Booster Deck. This deck contains extra cards to help you when you play.

Pick a Square: When the game begins, you'll find yourself standing on a square stone on top of a bubbling pit of hot sauce. Your opponents will each be standing on a stone as well. When it's your turn, click on one of the stones that appears in the hot sauce pit. Two of the squares surrounding the pit will light up. Click on the square to choose what kind of battle you will have—fire, water, snow, classic *Card-Jitsu*—or choose your element.

Choose a Card: If you land on an element square, you must play the element on that square. The highest card wins the battle. When it's your opponent's turn, that ninja will get to choose the element. If you land on a square with three elements on it, you'll get to decide which element you'll all be battling with.

Classic *Card-Jitsu*: If you choose the *Card-Jitsu* square, you will battle another player in the classic version of the game.

Watch Your Energy: If you lose a battle, you will lose one energy point. The player to hold on to their energy points the longest wins first place.

Every time you play, you will earn experience points. You'll earn more points the higher you place. If your opponent quits, you will still earn points, but you won't earn any points if *you* quit. As you collect points, you will earn a piece of your Ninja Fire Suit. You've mastered *Card-Jitsu Fire* once you've collected all four pieces of the suit. When you have the suit, you can challenge Sensei to earn a Fire Gem for your Amulet.

GAME TIP

Are you ready for a new wave of adventure? You'll need to think fast—and click even faster—to cross the water and ring the gong.

Boost Your Deck: The first time you enter the Water Dojo and talk to Sensei, he will give you extra water cards to help you when you play.

Know Your Goal: When the game begins, you'll be standing on a stone on top of a raging waterfall. You need to jump from stone to stone to get across the water and ring the gong. If you don't act fast enough, you'll fall over the edge of the waterfall and be out of the game.

Clear Stones with Cards: You can jump on stones to the front, left, right, or diagonally. Some stones are empty, but most will have either fire, water, or snow on them. To clear a stone so you can jump on it, choose one of the *Card-Jitsu* cards scrolling on the bottom of your screen. Fire clears snow, snow clears water, and water clears fire.

Try and Try Again: Let's say the stone in front of you has snow on it. You throw a fire card worth three points at it. The snow may melt a little, but there's still some left. Keep throwing fire cards until all the snow melts away.

Earn Your Suit: You will gain experience each time you play. The water suit consists of Wave Sandals, Waterfall Coat, Torrent Mask, and Helmet of Oceans.

GAME TIP

Once you earn your Water Suit, you can challenge Sensei to earn a Water Medal for your Amulet.

Igloo

The places that every penguin on the island calls home can be made even cooler with special furniture, decorations, and more. Find out all the possible ways you can decorate your igloo to really show off your personality.

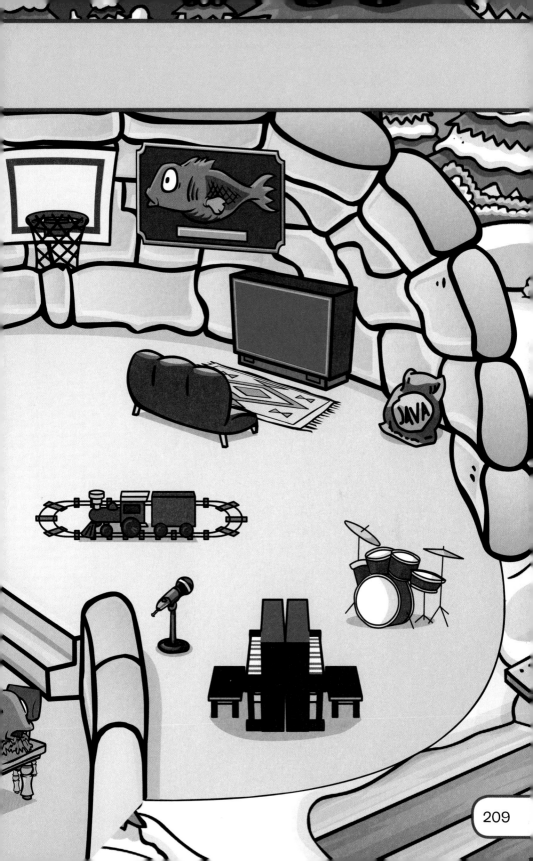

Igloo Basics

To create the igloo of your dreams, you'll need to know your way around the igloo icons. They're pretty simple once you start using them.

To get to your igloo, look at the blue toolbar on the bottom of your screen. Click on the 🏠 icon.

Once you're at your igloo, on the right-hand side, you'll see two icons: a 🔒 and a 📏. Click on the 🔒 to unlock your igloo. That means that your igloo is open to other penguins and will appear on the list of open igloos on the main page. Only unlock your igloo if you don't mind visitors!

Click on the 📏 to start decorating. You can choose a location for your igloo and decorate according to that theme.

Click on the menu at the top of your screen and you'll be able to see all of your furniture. All igloos come with furniture to start, but you can buy more with your coins.

Click on the 📔 to start shopping. You can find everything you need to decorate your space.

You can save up to twelve different igloo layouts that you can use at any time. When you save a design, you can choose whether your friends can see it or not.

Click on the 🏠 to upgrade your igloo. You can buy new flooring or choose a whole new design. You can save your designs so you can change the layout of your igloo whenever you like. Saved designs can be found by clicking 📦.

When you are finished making changes to your igloo, make sure you click on the 💾 icon to save all your changes.

I love to decorate my igloo with the exciting items that appear in each new catalog. If you place ninety-nine items in your igloo, you will earn a Stamp! Of course, that makes it very difficult to find your puffles, so you may want to clear up your clutter before too long.

AUNT ARCTIC SAYS

Decorating How-Tos

Let your igloo show off your own unique style. You can buy new items or use the free ones you've found to decorate with. Here's how to do it:

- Click on the 🖼 icon, then the 📦. You'll find all of your igloo items in here. The items in the box are arranged by category: furniture, stuff that hangs on walls, floor coverings, and puffle furniture.

- Choose the item you want in your igloo and then click on it. It will be dropped into the center of your room. Click on the item again and move your mouse to place it where you would like it, then click to drop it.

- You can rotate your item to face a different direction. Press ⬅ and ➡ to do so.

- Some items have cool hidden features. Click on an item and then press the up and down arrow keys on your keyboard to see if anything happens. Doing this will change the channels on a television set or light a fire in your fireplace. Experiment to see what else your stuff can do.

- Happy with your igloo decoration? Click the 💾 icon to save your changes.

- If you would like to remove an item from your igloo, simply drag it outside of your igloo when you are in edit mode. It will stay in storage until you need it again.

Awesome Igloo Items

Here are some of the items that can be found in igloos all over Club Penguin. You can find them in the Better Igloos catalog. If you don't see them in the current issue, check back in the future.

Confetti Blaster: This tube shoots a constant shower of confetti in your igloo. You can hide the tube behind a painting or other object so no one sees it.

Portal Box: Step inside this mysterious box to enter the Box Dimension.

Crystals: These glowing stones are peaceful as well as beautiful.

Radiant Rocker: Show your love of music with a glowing neon guitar.

Several times a year, Club Penguin holds igloo-decorating contests. I love to see how creative penguins get with their designs! You don't need to have dozens of items to win. What's important is to use your imagination! Anyone can enter—you can read all about them in *The Club Penguin Times*.

AUNT ARCTIC SAYS

Puffle Beanbag Chair: You can customize this comfy chair with different colors and fabric patterns.

Double Dunk Chair: What's better than eating a donut? Sitting on a giant one!

Waterfall Pond: Create a tranquil spot outside (or inside) your igloo with this lovely pond. It even has a koi fish swimming in it.

Ice Fishing Decal: Grab a fishing pole and go fishing without ever leaving home!

Disco Ball: Pair this with a Dance Floor, crank up the music, and hold the best igloo party ever!

What did the winter hat say to the scarf?

You hang around while I go on ahead!

Igloo Styles

In the Igloo Upgrades catalog, you'll find many different igloo styles to choose from. Here are some ideas for how to use them. But remember, the best igloo ideas come from your own imagination!

Dragon's Lair
You can fill this igloo with medieval furniture, of course, but it would also make a cool gothic dance club or a fab beauty salon.

Ice Castle
Give your puffles the royal treatment by turning this igloo into a Puffle Palace, or add tables and chairs to create a royal restaurant.

In Half Igloo
Make one side of this igloo for puffles and one side for penguins. Or you could use one half as a waiting area and the other as a dentist's office. Or simply do a different color on each side. Whatever you do, you'll have double the fun!

Estate Igloo

This spacious igloo is the perfect setting for a home movie theater. Set up lots of big screens and comfy couches and invite your buddies to come watch the show.

Gingerbread House

You can decorate this igloo to be the perfect holiday cottage. You could even turn it into a toy shop, complete with worktables and tons of toys.

Fishbowl

Host the world's greatest pool party in this igloo, or fill it with plants to create a fantastic aquarium.

Join the Community

As you now know, Club Penguin is filled with things to do, places to go, and penguins to see. But the island is a special place because of all the penguins who live, play, and work here—penguins just like you!

Becoming part of the community can be as easy as making a new friend or as involved as putting on a play at the Stage. Find out the many different ways to get into the action.

Meet Your Friends Online

It's easy to become buddies with penguins you meet on Club Penguin—and you can buddy your friends, brothers, and sisters, too.

Make a Plan: Talk to your friend before you both go on Club Penguin. Arrange to log in to the same server (such as Bigfoot) at the same time, and meet in a specific place (such as the Iceberg).

Send a Request: When you see your friend, click on the ⬤ icon on their Player Card. Your friend will get a postcard asking them to accept your buddy request. When they do, you'll be buddies! You can see if they're online, visit their igloo, and send them mail.

Keep Track: Click on the ⬤ icon on the bottom of your screen to access your friends. A yellow smiley face next to a penguin's name means that penguin is on the same server as you. Click on their name to see their Player Card. Then click on the ⬤ icon to find out where they are.

Say Hi: Click on the ✉ icon on your buddy's Player Card to send a postcard. Or, if you and your buddy are in the same place, type what you want to say in the toolbar on the bottom of your screen. Click on the 💬 icon and the words will appear in a speech bubble over your head.

Did You Know?: If the words you type don't appear on-screen, it means you are in Ultimate Safe Chat mode. Luckily, you can still communicate. Click on the 💬 icon all the way to the left of your toolbar. Then scroll up and over to see a bunch of phrases you can click on.

I Feel 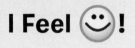!

When words can't express how you feel, say it with emotes! These little icons can show your mood (😃) or help you ask for what you want. (▷). To access them click on the winking smiley face on the left side of your toolbar. Then scroll up until you see the emote icon that you want and click on it. It will appear in the speech bubble above your head.

I enjoy using emotes so much that I've discovered seven secret emote shortcuts. They are: **E** + **I** = 🐚; **E** + **P** = 😺; **E** + **M** = 🪙; **E** + **N** = 🌙; **E** + **W** = 🎈. Hit **E** + **T** to get ♪ – with an extra sound! Try it and see what happens.

AUNT ARCTIC SAYS

222

If scrolling takes too long, you can use these keyboard shortcuts to choose an emote.

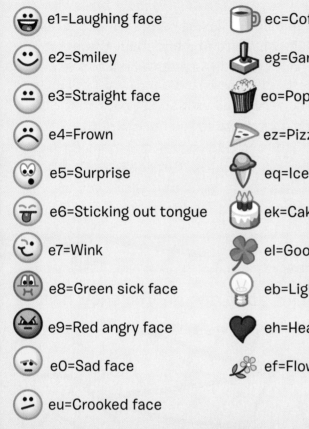

e1=Laughing face

e2=Smiley

e3=Straight face

e4=Frown

e5=Surprise

e6=Sticking out tongue

e7=Wink

e8=Green sick face

e9=Red angry face

e0=Sad face

eu=Crooked face

ec=Coffee cup

eg=Game

eo=Popcorn

ez=Pizza

eq=Ice cream

ek=Cake

el=Good luck

eb=Lightbulb

eh=Heart

ef=Flower

The Newspaper Needs You!

Every Thursday, a new issue of *The Club Penguin Times* hits the stands. You can read it by clicking on the newspaper on the top left of your screen. You'll find out about the latest happenings, learn about upcoming events, and discover new secrets.

Penguins just like you contribute to the newspaper, too. You can submit original jokes and riddles, and questions for Aunt Arctic to answer. Click on the words "Get Published" on the front page. That will take you to a link that allows you to submit your jokes and questions.

Where do penguins go to dance? The snow ball!

As editor in chief for *The Club Penguin Times* and writer for the "Ask Aunt Arctic" advice column, I am often asked by penguins how they can get their work into the newspaper. I get so many wonderful submissions each week, it's hard to decide what to publish. The number one piece of advice I can offer is be original! I am always looking for something interesting and new.

AUNT ARCTIC SAYS

Meet Aunt Arctic

When you help other penguins, it makes Club Penguin a better place for everyone!

Occupation: Aunt Arctic is the advice columnist and editor in chief of *The Club Penguin Times*. Each week she answers two questions in her "Ask Aunt Arctic" column. She loves keeping up on all the happenings on the island, which is why she's perfect for giving tips and secrets.

What You Might Be Surprised to Learn: If a reader asks Aunt Arctic a question and she's not sure of the answer, she'll find out—no matter what! If a penguin wants to know if you can make it to the end of every level of *Jet Pack Adventure* on one tank of fuel, she'll strap on a jet pack and investigate.

What She Can't Live Without: Her puffles!

Is It Possible to Meet Aunt Arctic?: Aunt Arctic is very busy with her writing, but she makes special appearances at the Anniversary Party and other events when she can.

Favorite Color: Green.

She Has a Sense of Humor: In 2009, Aunt Arctic played an April Fool's Day prank by convincing penguins to try to get one another to say "Grub!" in crowded places. It is still a popular Club Penguin expression.

The Club Penguin Times reveals a lot of secrets about the island. But do you want to know a secret about me? The next time you read the newspaper, try moving your mouse over my eyeglasses. Something shady just might happen . . .

AUNT ARCTIC SAYS

Club Penguin Parties

About once a month, Club Penguin throws an official island-wide party. These are celebrations you definitely don't want to miss. At a party, you can:

- look for free items.

- play new games.

- buy new backgrounds, outfits, or igloo items that go along with the party themes.

- go on a scavenger hunt to discover treasures or new places.

- meet famous penguins, such as Captain Rockhopper.

Don't Miss These Popular Parties!

Puffle Party: During the Puffle Party, the island gets transformed into a puffle paradise! There's an area set aside for every color puffle. In 2011, the Cove was turned into a pirate playground for red puffles, and purple puffles danced away in the Night Club.

Medieval Party: During the Medieval Party, you'll feel like you've stepped into another world. But the best thing about this party is the exciting adventures you can go on with rewards at the end.

Halloween Party: Gary the Gadget Guy loves this party because he gets to watch *Night of the Living Sled*, but you can also wear costumes, hunt for candy, and visit spooky spots at this haunted happening.

The Fair: The very first Fair was one of the most exciting parties ever to happen on Club Penguin, thanks to Captain Rockhopper. The pirate brought six new games to play at the party, including *Puffle Shuffle* and *Ring the Bell* (a test of strength). Penguins played games to earn tickets, and then traded in those tickets for cool prizes. It was so much fun that it's returned every year!

Free Items

Look for free items at official Club Penguin parties! Many free items come with a special action. To make it work, put on the special item and nothing else. Then go to your toolbar and click on "Dance" or "Wave" and see what happens.

Here's a look at a few free items and what they can do:

	Item	Action
	Propeller cap	Hover in midair
	Jet pack	Hover in midair
	Water wings	Swim
	Boom box	Break-dance
	Accordion	Play the accordion with sound
	Miner's helmet	Use a jackhammer
	Video camera	Record video

Fill Up Your Stamp Book

Every penguin has a Stamp Book. You can get to it through your Player Card. This special book holds Stamps that you earn by doing different kinds of things on Club Penguin. You can also see what you need to do to earn more Stamps.

Look at Your Book: Get to your Stamp Book by clicking on the ⊙ icon on your Player Card. Click on the round clasp on the right to open it up. Inside, you'll see tabs for the different categories of Stamps: Events, Activities, Games, Video Games, and Pins.

Earn Stamps: Scroll over each Stamp in the book to find out what you need to do to get one. See what Stamps you can earn by playing your favorite game. Or look under Events for fun challenges to try, like dancing in the Night Club with ten other penguins.

Keep Track: If you earn a Stamp while you're doing something, a message will pop up on your screen. Every time you open your book, you'll see what new Stamps you've earned.

Find Pins: The hidden pins you find will end up in your Stamp Book. That means you can add something new to your book every two weeks!

Customize Your Cover: Go to the cover of your book and click on the ✏️ icon on the bottom right of your screen. On the left, you'll see options for changing the color, pattern, and design of your Stamp Book. You can also drag up to six pins onto your cover to decorate it.

Check Out Your Buddies: You can see the Stamp Book of any player by clicking on the 🔘 icon on their Player Card. It's fun to look around and see what rare Stamps other penguins have collected.

Kids Helping Kids

Every day penguins help one another on Club Penguin—but they make a difference in the real world, too. Thanks to Club Penguin's Global Citizenship and Coins For Change programs, kids who play Club Penguin help children and the environment in many parts of the world.

How It Works

Each December, when the Coins For Change program begins, penguins raise virtual coins on Club Penguin by playing games or holding fund-raising parties. Then they donate their coins, deciding where their money will go. Club Penguin donates one million real-world dollars to the causes chosen by the players, and in 2011, Club Penguin donated an extra million, totaling two million dollars.

Who We've Helped

Coins For Change has benefited causes in places all over the world, including:

- Haiti, where a nutrition program feeds thousands of kids.

- Sri Lanka, where 20,000 kids displaced by war can find comfort at a Peace Center.

- Malawi, where children and their families receive medical care.

- Brazil, where local members of the community are trained to protect the rain forest.

And these are just some of the efforts supported by Club Penguin's players. It's proof that when penguins work together, we can help change the world!

Club Penguin Needs You!

There are more ways to pitch in and help make Club Penguin a fun place for everyone who visits. Here's a look at some cool things penguins have done—and things you can do right now!

Contribute to *The Club Penguin Times* and the Art Gallery: Submit jokes and questions to the newspaper. Or go to the Book Room to find out how you can submit your artwork to display in the art gallery!

Enter Contests: From time to time, you'll have a chance to share your special talents by entering contests for art, writing, igloo decorating, and more.

Take the Penguin Poll: Share your opinions about Club Penguin by clicking on "Community" on the home page and answering the latest poll question.

Be a Tour Guide: Help new penguins out by showing them around the island. Go to the Tour Guide booth in the Ski Village and take a test. If you qualify, you can become a guide.

Be a Secret Agent: Keep Club Penguin safe by going on missions and reporting penguins who are behaving badly to the moderator.

Make sure to read *The Club Penguin Times* every week or check the "What's New" blog to find out new ways to help. Things are always changing on Club Penguin!

Free Items

Item: _____ Date: _____

Item: _____ Date: _____

Item: _____ Date: _____

Item: _____ Date: _____

Item: _____ Date: _____

Item: _____ Date: _____

Item: _____ Date: _____

Item: _____ Date: _____

Item: _____ Date: _____

Item: _____ Date: _____

Item: _____ Date: _____

Item: _____ Date: _____

Item: _____ Date: _____

Item: _____ Date: _____

Item: _____ Date: _____

Item: _____ Date: _____

Item: _____ Date: _____

Index